Fly Fish the Trout Lakes

with

Jack Shaw

PHOTO CREDITS
B.C. Provincial Archives: 91; Canadian National Railway: 39; Heritage House: 6, 82, 91; Tourism B.C.: outside back cover, 46, 58, 74, 77, 80, 82, 92; Ron Boudreau: 1, 10, 27, 28, 29, 30, 31, 70; Jack Shaw: front cover, inside front, inside back cover, 8, 9, 12, 15, 19, 24, 58, 66, 77, 84, 94.

CANADIAN CATALOGUING IN PUBLICATION DATA

Shaw, Jack, 1916-
    Fly Fish the Trout Lakes

ISBN 0-919214-59-2

1. Fly fishing. 2. Trout fishing.
I. Title.
SH456.S53 1988   799.1'1   C88-091026-7

HERITAGE HOUSE
PUBLISHING COMPANY LTD.
Box 1228, Station A
Surrey, B.C. V3S 2B3

Printed in Canada

Dedication

To my wife, Dorothy, without whose
patience, encouragement and assistance
this book would not have been completed.

Acknowledgement

Much credit is due to the following friends
for assistance in preparing the text:
Mrs. Dianne Murphy, B.Sc.;
Mrs. Marion Belyk;
Mr. Heber Smith;
Mr. Don W. Holmes, M.Sc.

To Ralph Shaw my thanks for letting me
photograph the reels on page 12 from his Hardy
collection, and to Ron Boudreau who took the
excellent series of photos on pages 27 to 31,
among others.

Contents

Introduction

This book is the result of many requests for a handbook on fly fishing in lakes. Having taught fly-tying and casting for adult education programs for many years, and being a fishing consultant for a sporting goods store in the heart of the famous Kamloops trout fishing region, I agree that there is a great need for practical information on the art of fly fishing in lakes.

The more commonly practiced fly fishing in streams is so different in all aspects from lake fishing that a stream fly fisherman can be at a loss to understand lake waters and fishing therein. The purpose of this book, therefore, is to so fill a need. Even a novice can, with a little practice and observation, become proficient and get the most in relaxing enjoyment from the sport. A keen but observant mind, curiosity, a great deal of patience and practical experience can convert a novice into a skilled fisherman — or fisherwoman.

Fishing may be a truly family affair. Under parental guidance the first attempt is often with the age-old hook, line and worm in a small stream where a 4- to 7-year-old can come to little harm, and a fish of 7 inches talked of for days, growing to tremendous proportion with each telling.

For the next few years, Dad's old rod and reel is very useful. After a few weekends, with Dad patiently instructing and removing flies from clothing and even ears and neck, the novice becomes reasonably proficient in casting. True, there is one phenomenon which greatly lessens the numbers of fly fishermen of age 15 to 20 — the discovery of girls. But it is a passing affliction and after a few years the young fisherman, recovered, may again be seen in his old haunts, often with company.

Fly fishing is not difficult to master. It requires little in the way of physical strength. Observation and reasoning are most important assets. The ability to note available feed and its peculiarities and the movements of fish is as necessary as the ability to cast a fly.

In large bodies of water flies that are the bulk of the fishes' diet are almost entirely of aquatic origin. Terrestrials, or insects which live on land, are important only when a major hatch inadvertently is blown from land over the water. In streams, to the contrary, flies and insects of terrestrial origin are even more important than the aquatic insects.

Resorts and fishing camps are located on many of the popular lakes, offering various types of accommodation. Some have excellent dining room service while others offer the comforts of housekeeping cabins or camping facilities. Some even have small stores which carry necessities and fishing equipment. Boats are in most cases available.

Fishing mountain lakes is almost impossible without a boat of some type. With timber and brush growing to the water's edge there is no room for a back cast and in many cases there are shoal areas for some distance from shore on which sedge grass and rushes flourish. Chara weed, lily pads and many other types of vegetation are found in abundance, each species growing in its own particular type of aquatic environment.

Insects of many aquatic orders and many different species make their home in the abundant growth in the shallow shoal areas and the deeper water of these lakes. In B.C. it is these aquatic orders of insects that form the food chain on which the famous Kamloops trout of the rainbow species feeds to attain a large size and superb fighting ability. These are the qualities that make it the most sporting of the trout family to fly fishermen — or women.

In this work references made to the Kamloops trout apply, of course, to the rainbow as this trout is more commonly known in temperate zones of North America. But trout in general as they inhabit lake waters will respond to the strategies here recommended.

It is my sincere hope that the following material will improve your sport and make it more enjoyable.

There are over 16,000 lakes in B.C. While nearly 15,000 are less than one-half square mile in area, over 200 are five square miles or larger. Eight cover over 100 square miles each, including Quesnel which is 50 miles long and yields rainbow to over 25 pounds.

6

CHAPTER ONE

Rods

Four basic pieces of equipment are essential for fly fishing — rod, reel, line, and leader.

The rod has seen many changes over the years. Most recent of these have been in the materials involved in the manufacture of the rod blanks. Cane rods of a few years ago still have a small following, as a few people are not readily inclined to accept change and vehemently defend the merits of the traditional good quality cane. Glass, once the favorite of many and still very popular, has in recent years been replaced by graphite. The graphite rods have a small diameter, very light weight and a very high energy factor. They also have a much greater tolerance for a diversity of line weights.

I am of the old school but concede that graphite rods are superior in every way to anything I have used in the past. They justly deserve the popularity they have won.

Modern high quality hardware is likewise designed to give maximum durability with minimum weight. Most reel seats are of aluminum alloy, very light and durable. The better reel seats have a double lock nut system accommodating a wide range of reel sizes and holding them securely to the rod.

Guides on the better rods are of the finest quality. The first guide, in front of the handle, is usually known as a "bridge" guide. On fly rods this guide is called the "stripping" guide and is frequently made of a very hard metal that is a dark dull grey, virtually impervious to wear. The "tip top" and stripping guides take the bulk of wear from line friction. Grit and dirt adhering to a wet line has a considerable abrasive action and must travel through hardware (tops and guides) of hard enough material to withstand it. Otherwise the angler would be continually replacing worn ones to prevent injury to lines.

The guides situated between the stripping guide and tip top on light rods are of stainless steel wire and called "snake" guides, owing to the way in which the wire is bent to form the loop that contains the line. This design allows for maximum flexibility of the rod while maintaining light weight. Heavier rods, however, make use of the bridge-type guides, particularly in the butt section where maximum flexibility is not important.

The popular rods of today are made in two sections for convenience of transport. At one time rods were popular in three sections and are still favored in some areas. Rods of more than three sections are commonly referred to as pack rods because the short length of the unassembled rods makes them a favorite of backpackers and hikers.

Until recently it was almost impossible to build a rod of more than three sections that had good action and light weight. Metal ferrule systems of connecting the sections into a rod added considerable weight and stiffness. When you consider putting an 8- to 9-foot rod together in a number of sections, each joined by an unyielding metal connection 3 or 4 inches long, it can be understood how rod action becomes stiffer with each added ferrule.

With the comparatively new method of using tubular glass spigots forming the male end in the butt section and the natural hollow of the tip or following section forming the female part of the joint, little is lost in the way of action. This system of using the same material as the rod adds very little weight and maintains a great deal of action in the ferrule area. For this reason there is on the market today a selection of pack rods in four, five and even six sections having very acceptable action.

This action is the most important quality in any fly rod. Without it, casting a line any distance would be extremely difficult, if not impossible.

Action in a fly rod is that part of progressive resistance from tip to handle. In casting a line, this resistance is referred to as energy because

As the young boy at Lac Le Jeune illustrates, fly fishing is neither mysterious nor expensive and can be enjoyed by all ages. Two rainbow are cruising in front of him.

the rod's resistance to the weight of the line develops momentum when power is applied in a direction opposing the line's travel. Fly rods must have the correct weight of line for each individual model of rod.

To explain this principle more fully, let's assume we are individuals of average strength. At our disposal there is a cannon ball of 20 pounds, a table tennis ball of one-tenth ounce, and a baseball of 5 ounces. In an effort to throw the cannon ball we find all the energy we have fails to move it any appreciable distance.

We now try the same experiment with the table tennis ball of one-tenth ounce. We find that we fail again to attain any great distance. We have the strength or energy but the ball has not sufficient weight to utilize this energy and convert it to momentum to carry it very far. Now we repeat the performance with the 5-ounce baseball and find the ball will travel a great distance with the same amount of effort as applied to the other items. While spherical volume has some bearing on our experiment it is not of enough significance to be worthy of consideration.

I hope this analogy explains why a light (low energy) rod requires a line of lighter weight than a more powerful (high energy) rod.

Many fishermen fail to attach enough importance to the proper selection of rods. A fly rod suitable for fishing rivers is not necessarily a good rod for lake fishing. The reverse is also true. The two environments are totally different because fish in each react as the situation and natural feed requires.

Since there is little, if any, natural current in a lake, fish are inclined to be rather slow and lazy in feeding, taking time to look things over more than in fast water. For this reason very fine leaders must be used in lakes,

Good equipment properly used not only gives much pleasure but also results in catches such as the Kamloops trout below.

particularly lakes of clear water. While colored waters are more forgiving, it is still an advantage to use the lighter leaders.

Lighter leaders demand light action rods if one is to handle the strike — especially the sometimes violent attack — of a large fish. The resistance of a powerful rod is more often than not responsible for a broken leader on the strike. For this reason, light action rods are more desirable than rods of medium to heavy action. I prefer a rod that will handle a #7 line; but one that will effectively cast a #6 line is also acceptable.

A #8 line-rod combination I find a little heavy. In order to consistently survive the strike on the latter combination, 6-pound-test leader tippets seem the lightest that are practical.

I frequently hear the argument that a powerful rod will punch a line into the wind far more effectively than a light rod. I heartily agree. If punching a line into the wind is a person's pleasure, by all means be my guest. For myself I enjoy playing a lively fish and I have a warm spot in my heart for the odd large fish that comes to my fly. They do not come that often that I'm about to lose it if light rods and leaders will give me an advantage. Seldom have I found it necessary to cast into any appreciable wind. The occasion does arise, however, if more than one person fishes from a boat. Then one of them is usually stuck with casting into the wind.

When this situation does arise don't try for a long cast, but rather a moderate one that could normally be handled with ease. By keeping the rod low (sidearm), the line is on the water before the wind can get control and blow it back at you. With a little practice a very respectable cast can be made into a fairly strong wind.

At this time a word of caution: When two or more people are fly casting from the same boat, whether or not it is windy, it is an advantage to wear glasses of some kind. A bad cast or a changeable wind and an eye can be lost to a fly.

It is much better for all concerned if each person has his or her own boat. It allows for much more individual freedom, there is less danger of accidental hooking of one another, and twice as much water can be covered. In addition, there is nothing lost socially. Conversations in moderate tones can be carried on comfortably over some distance since sound travels readily over lake water.

The author's fishing punt, his home made "wet-weather" seat near the bow. (See page 69.)

## CHAPTER TWO

The Fly Reel

The basic function of a fly reel is to store a sufficient amount of backing and a fly line, smoothly paying out line and retrieving as required. It should, therefore, be a very simple mechanism consisting of a drum, or spool, to hold line and a body to encase the friction device and support the axle on which the drum turns. The friction device, or drag, need not be adjustable. The only purpose it serves is to prevent overrunning or a backlash when the line is pulled rapidly from the drum.

Close tolerance between the reel body and drum is essential. Too much clearance allows the line to foul by getting between drum and body on occasion. Besides being a nuisance, this defect is a common cause of damage to fly lines. Reel drums that have rivets protruding to the inner surface where line is stored should be avoided for obvious reasons.

A one-piece drum designed for fast line pick-up has a small hub. The sides are not parallel but taper from the outer limit, becoming narrow at the hub. This design allows the small hub to quickly build a diameter when the line is wound. As the diameter builds, the circumference quickly increases, permitting a rapid recovery of line when required. This feature is only found in the more expensive reels.

For fly fishing on lakes the simplest construction in a fly reel is the most desirable. The foregoing statement, however, is not intended to imply that the least expensive is the best. Some of the finest quality reels are very simple mechanically, while some of the least expensive are mechanically elaborate and complicated.

The simplest type of fly reel is referred to as a "single action" reel because the handle is fixed directly to the spool. One revolution of the handle turns the drum one revolution.

Multiplier reels have about the same outward appearance as the single action. The difference is mechanical and not too obvious unless the spool is removed from the body of the reel. It will then be noticed that there is a system of gears which permits the drum to revolve more than once with

A reel is used primarily to store line, with single action the favorite of fly fishermen. The three above were made by Hardy, a firm well known to anglers.

each turn of the handle. While the multiplier may be an excellent reel for some types of fishing, it is not recommended for lakes where the trout are large and gamey.

In defence of this statement, let me explain. If one never has a fish on large enough to run out backing or take line off the reel when using recommended leaders of 4- or 6-pound test, there will probably be no difficulty. However, we cannot guarantee that an angler will catch only small fish, and I doubt if anyone would wish us to. Aren't we all looking for that big one?

The tension that builds up in starting the multiplier reel by pulling line off the spool would part even very strong leaders since the gear ratio is about two and a half or three to one. That is, for each turn of the handle the drum will revolve two and a half or three times. A full spool, working through the gear system, requires a certain amount of energy to turn it by pulling off line. As line is removed and the diameter of line on the spool becomes smaller, the leverage becomes greater until the leader can no longer survive such punishment. As a consequence, that large fish you came for is lost.

Another type of reel is the automatic which is spring operated. It has no handle on the spool but operates by a lever which is a brake. The line being pulled off the reel winds the spring, or the spring can be wound by turning the outer housing which is built into the side of the reel body. By depressing the lever the spring turns the spool, recovering the line.

A fish is played by depressing the brake lever, letting the fish fight the spring tension. As the fish tires and gives to the pull of the spring, it is automatically wound to the net with no more effort or skill on the part of the fisherman than the ability to hold the brake lever down.

Models of these reels that I have seen have small capacity, with little or no room for backing. I feel this feature makes them unsuitable for lake fishing.

In summary, then, a reel is used primarily to store line. Fish are played by hand. Line that is retrieved while playing a fish is either coiled in the hand or let fall to the bottom of the boat.

When large fish are encountered and backing is stripped from the reel, then the fish is "put on the reel." This expression means that the backing is recovered by playing the fish with the reel. The reason is that the backing is prone to tangle badly unless used in this manner. Once the fly line is started again on the spool it is optional whether the play is continued on the reel or by hand. I favor playing by hand whenever possible as I seem to have a more delicate and sensitive control, being able to "feel" the fish better and predict a move in time to react. This feel, too, adds to the joy of fishing.

Reels should always be filled to within one-quarter inch of the rim of the spool, allowing faster line recovery owing to the maximum circumference. Also the maximum volume of backing is at times a great comfort.

There have been reams written and hours of discourse on the relative merits of various reels. Balance between reel and rod has been the subject of much of it. It leads one to believe that fishing with a reel that does not balance the rod is virtually impossible. Nothing could be more incorrect. If one has no reel at all, apart from the inconvenience because of lack of a place to store unused line without tangling after the fish is on, I doubt that it would be missed greatly.

If you fish with a reel that is too heavy there will be a tendency to move your hand back until, in some cases, the heel of the hand will be directly above the reel. This condition, however, will be found only in cases of extreme imbalance. More often the reel is too light and there is an inclination to move forward until the thumb and first finger are off the handle entirely. This problem can be corrected by weighting the butt of the rod if it is not practical to use a heavier reel.

Ideally, the thumb should rest on top of the handle about an inch from the forward end. This position indicates perfect balance, giving the greatest comfort and control.

## CHAPTER THREE

Lines

Often the success of a fishing trip depends on the selection of a line.

Fly lines are designed to present the various types of flies in a natural manner and come in a variety of styles, types, colors and qualities. Good quality lines may be expensive but perform superbly. If you select the correct weight of line for your rod you are assured of pleasure and satisfaction for many years.

Inexpensive lines, by contrast, do not perform consistently. Too often, an inferior sinking line seems reluctant to do so and a supposedly floating line cannot decide whether to float or sink. The result is a line that has portions under water and portions that want to abide by the manufacturer's claim that it will float.

Sinking lines, the most useful of all fly lines in fishing lakes, are used to fish with imitations below the surface and are made in three classes — slow sink, fast sink and extra fast sink. These classes refer to the density of the lines and are in no way related to their weight. The density of the line is usually indicated by numbers — the slow sinker #1, fast sinker #2, extra fast sinker #3. Extra fast sinker #3 is also referred to as HiD, meaning high density.

The next line is referred to as a sinking tip line. This line is built with a main body which floats but a 10-foot portion of the end that sinks. The sinking tip is very useful on shoal areas and in shallow lakes. It allows the fisherman ample time to work a fly effectively in water 5 - 15 feet deep. It is particularly effective where it is desirable to imitate an insect rising from the bottom to emerge at the surface. The floating portion gives a natural lift to the fly as it is retrieved through the water.

The floating line rides the surface tension of the water and is used with flies that are naturally on or near the surface. It is used for presenting terrestrial imitators of insects that fish feed on, and is also very useful in fishing emerging nymphs and pupae a few inches to a foot or so under the surface.

Modern fly lines are built with a fabric core and various types of

To the author, sinking lines are the most useful of all lines for lake fishing. Good quality ones are expensive but will give years of satisfaction, typified by the above 4-pound Sheridan Lake rainbow.

braiding. Some are braided solid, many — particularly floating line core — are braided hollow. The core is covered with a smooth plastic material. It is the density of this material that controls the buoyancy of a fly line. The coating of some dry fly lines is advertised as being a controlled mass of tiny air bubbles. This feature greatly increases the floating life of a line. (Floating lines that become grimy with oil, dirt or algae from the water are prone to sink until cleaned and dressed with a good dry line dressing.)

Many materials are used to accomplish the control of line density to give the fly fisherman the right sinking speed to meet his requirements. I have a sinking line that is impregnated with metal particles in order to add to its density.

Assuming a speed of three seconds per foot of line, the effective depths of the three densities of line are: Slow sink #1 will work water to about 15 feet deep; fast sink #2 is useful to about 25 feet; while the extra fast sink #3 is effective to around 40 feet.

Except in rare instances the extra fast sinking line is not particularly useful in lake fishing. At a depth of 40 feet, a 60- or 70-foot cast will be very close to the boat at effective depth, owing to the arc of the fly as it drops through the water with the rod tip as the pivot point.

All quality lines are made in various tapers, the most common of which are the double taper and shooting taper. Double-taper lines are built with a level belly section with a tapered tip about 10 feet long on each end, the entire line being 90 feet long.

Shooting tapers are built with the maximum weight spread over the forward 25 feet of line. The tip, or forward end, is tapered for about 8 or 10 feet, the following 15 feet is made with a short section followed by a taper to a small diameter level running line. Shooting tapers are commonly made in 35-yard lengths.

The dimension of these lines varies with different manufacturers. They are also made with varying weight dispersion for specific purposes and named to denote the purpose for which they were designed — bass-bug taper and salt-water taper, to name two.

Rods of different energies require lines of suitable weight to use this energy efficiently and convert it to momentum. (Momentum is the speed at which a line must travel in order to keep it airborne over the required distance, an action referred to as the "cast.")

Fly line manufacturers in recent years have devised a system of numbers that enables the fisherman to select weights of lines that will fit each particular rod. For instance, a rod which works well with a line of #7 weight in a particular brand, design or density, will work the same with any other brand as long as the AFTMA number is #7.

The designation AFTMA means: American Federation of Tackle Manufacturers Association. The standard they use is:

# 1	— 60 grains	# 7	— 185 grains
# 2	— 80 grains	# 8	— 210 grains
# 3	— 100 grains	# 9	— 240 grains
# 4	— 120 grains	#10	— 280 grains
# 5	— 140 grains	#11	— 330 grains
# 6	— 160 grains	#12	— 380 grains

A few grains of tolerance are allowed on either side of these figures. These weights are based on what is considered to be the false casting portion of the line; namely, the forward 30-foot length.

Floating lines cast more easily and require less finesse than sinking lines owing to their volume in relation to density. The large diameter for the weight allows the line to be more buoyant in the air as it travels. Sinking fly lines, being more dense, have smaller diameters in the same weight range and therefore lose, to some extent, the advantage of air buoyancy. As a consequence, more exactness is required when casting.

Color of fly lines is to some degree a matter of personal preference. Sinking lines are usually medium to dark shades of green or brown. I do not entirely endorse the manufacturers' choice of color shade for sinking lines, but there seems to be little choice as I have never found the color I prefer. I feel a sinking line should be the shade of the vegetation in the lakes, ideally a rather yellow olive of medium tone. Being a natural color to the fish, it would be less likely to arouse suspicion. Another consideration is that suspended materials in the water such as algae and minerals create color, having a degree of influence on what the fish sees as it peers at the surface.

Floating lines are popular in paler shades — ivory, white, grey, blue, green and pink — although a few are produced in darker shades of brown, grey and green.

In lake fishing i find the pale pink, white, ivory and palest blue the most useful. This preference is because Nature protects fish from predators swimming below them by coloring the undersides to blend with their background, in this case the sky.

Since a fly line on the surface as seen by a fish has the sky as a background, the palest of colors are the best choice for maximum camouflage of the line.

To the fisherman these pale colors are most visible because he sees the line from above and has the dark water as a background. Since the pale shades stand out so clearly, viewed from the fisherman's eye level, it may be a surprise to be told they are least visible to the fish.

I have frequently been asked about the breaking test of fly lines. I have never seen any manufacturers' specifications and have had no reason to conduct tests of my own. The strength of a fly line is of little importance because it will assuredly be far, far stronger than the leader used between it and the fly.

## CHAPTER FOUR

Leaders

The leader is usually a nylon product commonly called monofilament, made specifically for attaching to fly lines between the line and the fly to reduce visibility to the fish. The line end is quite coarse, thinning to finer diameters at the fly end. This thinning is referred to as "taper." Better leaders are quite stiff in the heavy end, or butt section, becoming more limp at the fly end, or tip. This type of construction aids the unfolding, or laying out, of the leader in a straight line and permits the unrestricted movement of the fly.

The most popular lengths are 7½ feet and 9 feet. Tip diameters are designated in both pounds breaking strain and X numbers, and are also frequently given in thousandths of an inch. The latter varies widely depending on the manufacturer.

Following is the scale commonly found on packaged leaders which now also carry metric weight and measure designations:

Pound Test	X Designation
6	0x
5	1x
4	2x
3	3x
2½	4x
2	5x
1½	6x

Unfortunately, this scale tells only part of the story. Quality of leaders and leader material varies widely. Some leaders become quite weak when wet, others lose a great deal of their strength after an initial stretch, while still others are greatly weakened by a knot. In addition, an inconsistent diameter is not uncommon.

A leader fresh from the package or taken off the reel after having been coiled for some time will retain a "set," or spring-like coils. They must be removed by stretching the leader if it is to work properly. If undue pressure seems to be required it is best to hold about 2 or 3 feet taut and work it rapidly over one's pant leg. By working the entire leader in this manner it will soon lay out satisfactorily.

Some fishermen prefer to build their own tapered leaders by knotting short lengths of monofilament to a prescribed formula. I have used them and admit they have some merit. Longer leaders can be used because the weight can be placed to better advantage. Also, by properly combining hard and soft material, they can be made to unfold to suit the individual.

There are some drawbacks, however, that I consider serious. Because short pieces of material are used, knots are required, often three or four. They have an embarrassing habit of slipping, especially when it is most advantageous to the fish. As a result you lose both fish and fly, and too often it is the last fly you have that is working at the time! Also, I have never been able consistently to keep from fouling the leader on the knots. It always seemed to me I was spending too much time untangling leaders or rebuilding them to make the advantages worth the effort.

One aspect of leaders that can puzzle a beginner is the correct strength, or test. How often have I heard someone say, "There are large fish in such-and-such a lake. I need a 6- or 8-pound-test leader."

How inexperienced that person is! Fish don't become large because they are stupid! If you cannot survive the strike on 2-, 3- or, at maximum, 6-pound-test leader it would be better to change your rod for one light enough to give with the fish when it strikes.

Many times I have had a fish refuse a fly on 4-pound-test leader and take readily on 2-pound-test. True, I lose a few fish and a few flies, but I land more than I lose. This compromise is much better than not having them strike.

I find the best leader for all round use is a tapered one of 6-pound

A 4-pound rainbow is a challenge to both tackle and angler.

test, 9 feet long. During late summer and early fall, after much fishing pressure, it is a distinct advantage to add a "tippet" of 4-pound test, 2 or 3 feet long. This addition will result in a leader about 11 or 12 feet long, increasing the distance from line to fly and adding to the success of late season fishing.

(A tippet is a piece of leader material that is knotted to the end of a regular leader to extend the length or reduce tip diameter. It also considerably extends the life of a tapered leader while retaining the advantages of the taper. The main leader being tapered becomes quite thick after a few inches have been used up by changing flies, and thus is more visible. The tippet maintains diameter and test strength every time the fly is changed until it is used to the point where it is cut off and a new piece added.)

Some difficulty may be experienced in laying out a leader of this length. By using a slightly shorter cast this problem is easily overcome and does not affect the advantage gained by the longer tippet.

Leaders and leader materials come in a wide range of colors and shades. There are also leaders that are called camouflage; that is, they have a number of colors alternately spaced and blended over their length. I have never been happy with them in fishing lake waters, but admit that in rivers and streams they may have some merit.

Over the years I have found certain colors of leader and leader material consistently out-perform all others. The color of water fished has some bearing on the color used.

Water color can be divided into three basic groups, governed by the type of material suspended in the water. Algae usually produce a yellow to yellowish green color. Bog type lakes tend to be colored by tannin from wood bark and are slightly brownish, while very clear lakes are often very slightly blue green.

Matching leader color to water is a distinct advantage. Avoid dark shades. The very palest of yellow, mist blue and brown are most useful. As already mentioned in the chapter on leaders, while color may appear quite distinct from above the water, it must be remembered that the dark bottom offers a greater contrast than the sky. What has meaning is the way a fish views color against the light of the sky.

Tea and coffee have been used for coloring leaders for many years. Just leave the material overnight in the beverage. A little experimenting will soon give an idea of strength of liquid to use for the desired tint.

In conclusion, remember always to use the very finest leader your skill and equipment will permit.

## CHAPTER FIVE

Knotting and Splicing

The Blood Knot is used for joining leader materials. Tippets are tied to tapered leaders in this way and built-up leaders make use of it.

With newer leader materials that have very small diameters for their

test strength this knot requires a small drop of glue. It is applied after the knot is tied and just before being pulled tight. After tightening wipe off excess glue and clip off the tag ends.

One end may be left the desired length to be used for a second, or dropper, fly if desired.

The Improved Cinch Knot is the most commonly used knot for fastening fly to leader, being quick and simple to tie. It uses a minimum of materials and is reasonably secure.

Here again the new leader materials create a problem — excessive

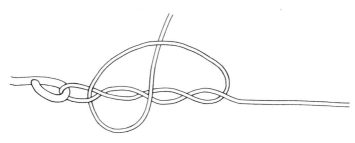

tightening of the knot. Under pressure of the knot's own turns the main leader is cut, giving the impression of poor knot strength when, in fact, actual knot strength is excellent. This problem is easily remedied by going twice through the eye of the fly, then tie as usual.

The Dropper Knot is a common means of forming a loop at any point along

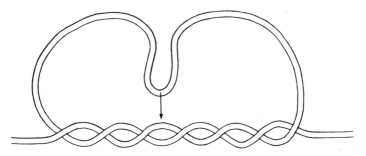

a leader to which a dropper may be tied for use with a second fly.

The Nail Knot is one method of tying a leader to a fly line. It can be used only on fly lines built with a hollow core, as are most popular top grade lines today.

This method has the advantage of the leader coming from the center of the line. Being very compact, it allows the join to pass easily through the tip top and guide, a great advantage when using very long leaders. A bulky knot may stop the leader at the rod tip with the fish remaining out of reach.

This knot requires the use of a sewing machine needle with a large eye and a #15 or #16 crochet hook.

The crochet hook is worked up the core of the line for about a half inch, the line bent at right angles and the hook pushed out the side. With the hook point towards the line, the tip of the leader is doubled back a few inches. The resulting loop is then taken with the hook and pulled through.

Continue pulling the leader through until there is about 4 inches of the butt section protruding from the side of the line. Tie the knot as il-

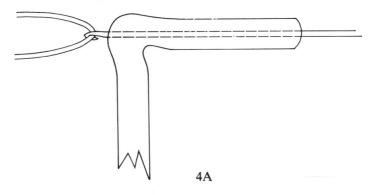

4A

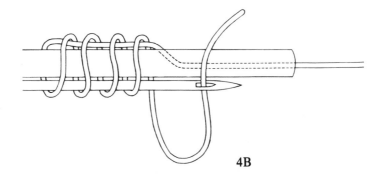

4B

lustrated in 4B, using the needle to pull the end under. Keep the knot as close as possible to where it emerges from the side of the line. Tighten by pulling hard on the loose end and the leader.

Splicing line to backing is very critical. If it is not done properly the purpose of the backing is defeated. The join must be able to pass smoothly through the guides going out and again on the retrieve.

The illustrated procedure is simple, extremely compact and secure. As with the nail knot, the only tool required is a #15 or #16 crochet hook. The hook is worked up the core of the line for five-eighths or three-quarters of an inch and pushed out the side as illustrated in 4A. A 5- to 6-inch loop of 6-pound-test monofilament for a #15 hook (4-pound for a #16) is taken with the hook and pulled through the core extending from the end of the line about 2 or 3 inches as shown in 5A.

The braided backing material (15- or 18-pound test) is frayed with a needle for about an inch. The frayed portion is divided as shown in 5B,

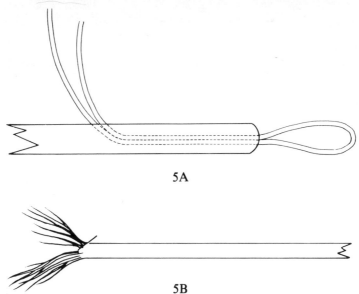

5A

5B

5C

and half of it cut off close as possible to the main line. The remaining half is put through the monofilament loop extending from the end of the fly line and doubled back on itself. The ends of monofilament protruding from the side of the line are used to draw the loop back through the core of the line, pulling the backing into the line's center and out the side. A knot is then tied in the end of the backing and a little glue spread on an inch or two of backing between the fly line and the knot. The fly line is then worked up the backing to the knot. Stretch the portion of fly line through which the backing passes to lock the backing into the line. The knot (5C) serves as greater insurance against losing the line.

From streams and lakes such as McConnell, below, B.C. anglers take about 5 million rainbow a year. Some 300,000 B.C. citizens — or 10 per cent of the population — spend an average of 18 days a year fishing in fresh water.

CHAPTER SIX

Casting

Now that we have some understanding of rods and lines insofar as weight of line and energy of rod is concerned, learning to cast will not be difficult. For now let's assume that the rod is simply a tool with which we cast a line. It is a great deal more, but for the present this analogy will meet our needs.

Energy applied to the rod handle travels up the rod to the tip where the weight of the line offers resistance. As the energy in the rod overcomes the resistance of the line, the line moves in the direction of the force, or energy. As energy transfers from the rod to the line it takes the form of speed, or momentum. Just before the line comes to rest, power is applied to the rod handle in the opposite direction and the line again moves in the direction to which the power is applied.

The distance the line travels depends on the energy applied to the rod and the ability of the line to utilize it efficiently.

To begin casting, imagine yourself standing beside a huge clock face, the rod held at the twelve o'clock position, thumb on the top of the handle and elbow close to the side. Hand and forearm will be at right angles to the body, the hand at the center of the imaginary face.

Now, move the rod to the eleven o'clock position, then back to the one o'clock position. This is the angle through which the rod should move under power when casting. Repeat a few times until you become familiar with these positions.

After attaching the reel and line to the rod, run out about 20 feet of line beyond the rod tip. A short piece of leader material with about an inch of pipe cleaner tied to the end will give much the same action as a fly and be quite safe to use. It is not advisable to use a line without a leader as the end will become frayed and pop like a whip, damaging the line severely if continued.

Before we cast, let's see if your equipment is assembled correctly. Assuming you are right handed, the reel handle should be on your right

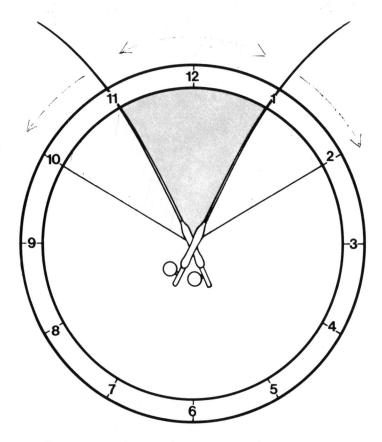

When casting, apply power only between eleven o'clock and
one o'clock. Do not apply power into the shaded area. Allow
the rod to drift into this area while awaiting line travel.

side, on the butt end of the rod, behind your hand. In this position it is
not likely to catch loose line you may be holding in your left hand. The
line should be coming off the spool at the bottom of the reel. This position
keeps the line far enough away from the rod to give your hand freedom
on the handle and permits better control of the line.

With the line laid out in front of you, take a few feet of line off the
reel and hold it in your left hand — provided you are right-handed.

Drop the rod to the ten o'clock position and take up any slack line.
Move the rod smartly to one o'clock. The line will move to the rear and
just before it straightens move the rod briskly to the eleven o'clock position. Continue this brisk back and forth motion between eleven and one
o'clock and the line should smoothly flow back and forth. Should it move
jerkily let the rod coast slightly past eleven and one o'clock, but remember
that power is applied only between the eleven and one o'clock positions.

After you have the line moving smoothly back and forth and feel it
is under control you are now ready to let out more. There is some difficul-

Holding line while
preparing to cast.

Starting the
back cast.

Holding line
to retrieve.

ty in coiling line in the hand to start with so just let it fall on the floor or ground, being careful not to step on it as it could be easily damaged.

You now have about 20 feet of line on the ground in front of you. Strip another 10 feet off the reel and let it lie at your feet. (Good fly line is not likely to tangle.) Now holding your line in the left hand start the 20 feet in motion. After one or two casts let a few feet of the coiled line slide through your left hand on the forward cast only. Stop the line sliding through your hand before it loses too much momentum and at the same time start the back cast, adding a little more power. More line can be let out on every forward cast until the desired length is reached.

There are now two things to consider: the time it takes the end of the line to travel from point A to point B (the forward and rear extremities travelled by the fly) and the amount of energy required to move the increasing weight of line over this distance. Hence, as more line is paid out, more power must be applied to the rod. At the same time you must wait longer for the line to straighten out before starting it back again. Take your time and don't get too anxious to get out a mile of line. A good short cast is always better than a bad long cast!

Going back on the back cast.

Here I might suggest that you watch your upper arm. Don't let the elbow drift back and forth. This drifting not only kills the rod action but also allows the rod to tip back beyond the one o'clock position. As a consequence, the line will hit the ground or water behind you, killing the momentum and ruining your cast. If this problem occurs, try holding a book to your body with the elbow while casting. It will help to solve the drifting problem.

Keep in mind, however, that letting the rod drift slightly beyond the angle of the power application, while waiting for the line to travel, will aid the smooth flow of rod and line. The result is a more graceful, effortless cast.

If you follow closely the foregoing instructions, in a short time "false casting" should be easy. (It is called false casting because the line does not touch the water while it is paid out to the desired distance. Hitting the water with line prior to the final presentation may be very frightening to the fish. It will, in fact, frequently scare them away, particularly late in the season after heavy fishing pressure has made them spooky.)

Starting the forward cast.

The forward cast.

Working the fly.

The presentation.

Playing the fish.

Presentation is the final move that lays the line, leader and fly on the water. Laying out a good line has a great advantage and is not difficult if a few points are practiced.

As we have seen, the false cast gets the line in motion and extends it to the desired length. On the forward cast, after the final application of power, allow the rod tip to drop to the natural horizon (where water and shore come together). From this position the line will lay out straight just above the water and then drop the remaining few inches upon it with very little disturbance.

Should the fly come back on the leader with the leader looped on the water, the solution is to drop the rod tip a little lower. The problem is caused by the fly and the leader straightening out above the water. As the fly hits the end of travel it is snapped back, landing on the water beside the line and the leader which then form a large loop in the water.

Should the line land heavily on the water, curling at the end, hold the rod tip up more on the final cast. This type of bad cast is caused by driving the line down too far, causing it to hit the water before straightening out. Do not try for very long casts before the technique has been mastered, then lengthen the cast only gradually. With a little practice a very nice line can be laid out.

A considerable length of dry fly line can be picked up off the water, false cast, then again presented. Begin by holding the rod horizontally with the water, drawing the slack line into the rod. At the same time lift the rod in the horizontal position to about shoulder height and, without pause, snap the tip of the rod up and back to the one o'clock position. From there continue as with a normal cast.

Wet, or more correctly, sinking lines cannot be handled in this way but must be fished out to within a few feet of the leader before being taken from the water and cast again.

Problems in casting are not hard to correct if the cause is known.

Hitting the water on the false cast is the result of applying power beyond the proper casting angle. This power drives the line down rather than straight out.

Hitting the rod with the line is often the result of rod and line moving in the same plane. The rod should move in an elongated oval — back on the outside of the oval, forward on the inside. Eight to ten inches between the two planes is sufficient.

A lazy looping cast with frequent hitting of the rod with the line could be caused by insufficient power being applied to the rod.

Knots in the leader are called "windknots." They usually are caused by trying to cast a few extra feet, making the cast, then moving the body and/or arm forward. To correct this error, move the body and/or arm forward first, then cast.

## CHAPTER SEVEN

Flies

The most common flies commercially available are based on old English patterns. There is no doubt that they were originally tied to imitate specific insects.

In many cases the original pattern, as to material and size, has been lost. Colors, too, have suffered to some extent. Availability of material and the demand for speed in production to keep costs down have further been responsible for their mutation. Wide variance in color of such natural material as fur and feathers contributed greatly to this catastrophe.

The hooks these old patterns were tied on were made by hand. If any two hooks were identical it was purely accidental. For this reason until the modern era the term "standard pattern" was at best extremely vague. The only true and dependable standard was the natural insect.

Old patterns were largely tied to represent terrestrial (living on land) insects, or terrestrial stages of aquatic insects. It was not until comparatively recent times that other stages of insect development were represented for angling. In England even today anything other than a dry fly is referred to as a lure rather than a fly.

Flies can be divided into categories in terms of what they represent such as dry fly, wet fly and nymph. Each of them can again be placed in order of imitator or attractor and divided into classes that refer to the mechanical construction such as hair wing, fan wing, bi-visible, variant and spent wing.

Dry flies, as the name implies, are those flies that are fished on the surface, the fish having to rise to take this offering.

Natural imitators work well when hatches are not too prolific. If a hatch is very large a close imitation has too much natural competition. At these times it is better to use an attractor type that is close to the natural form but not the color. Very like the little boy and the bowl of apples. If there is a nice red apple in a bowl of drab-colored ones there is no doubt which one will be taken. It is still an apple, but it stands out from its companions.

Like the little boy, a fish has no inhibitions and will also be attracted to the "red apple."

Wet flies are those that are used below the surface. They represent such insects as some species of sedge flies, damsel flies and others that swim to the bottom to deposit eggs on sticks and stones. Imitations of fresh water shrimp, leeches and snails are also called wet flies. This terminology is always a matter of wonder on my part, for at no time in the life cycle of the last three organisms are they terrestrial. So why call this representation "flies"?

Nymphal and pupal stages of insects are, in angling circles, usually grouped together under the heading of nymphs. This definition may not be correct, but the accepted term has been developed over the years for simplicity.

Terrestrial forms of aquatic insects that swim to the bottom to deposit eggs on sticks and stones enclose an air bubble about their body. Aquatic insects that are air breathers also carry air in bubbles which reflect silvery light somewhere about their body. Notable among these are the water boatmen and backswimmers.

Hard shelled insects — those with an exoskeleton — also reflect light to some extent off the curved portions of their body segments. This reflection is the reason for the success of tinsel ribbing in some flies.

There is also another cause of air bubbles on aquatics that is often overlooked by even the most experienced fly angler. This is a process whereby aquatic plants convert light to oxygen in the form of very tiny bubbles that rise to the surface in little strings like tiny pearls. Fresh water shrimp and damsel fly nymphs that move through and about the weeds will on occasion gather these bubbles about their bodies, usually on bright sunny days when the process is at a peak.

Often when an angler uses a fly with a furry body, he will catch a fish on the first cast or two, thereafter it may no longer produce. The reason is that the natural insects are carrying these tiny oxygen bubbles. The furry body of the imitation, having some natural oil in the hair, on the first few casts will retain air. While these bubbles are trapped the imitation fly is a success. After the fish has mouthed it, however, the air bubbles are gone and the imitation no longer has the appearance of a natural fly. Thereafter it is unproductive.

Whether an insect evolves from egg to larva to pupa to terrestrial, or from egg to nymph to terrestrial, the life span is far longer in the aquatic stages. Many spend as much as three years in the nymphal state before emerging as a terrestrial. Some species of dragonfly nymphs spend up to five years in the nymphal form. By contrast, the winged, or terrestrial, insect has a life span measured in hours. It is therefore easy to understand why the nymphal stage is likely to be the most productive imitation.

Because nymph and pupa forms of aquatics are seldom seen, they are rarely recognized by the angler — probably the reason for so few even reasonably close commercial imitations. In fact, the really successful nymphal and pupal patterns are not available commercially.

## CHAPTER EIGHT

Feeding Habits

The famous Kamloops, or rainbow, trout is an insect eater. So are most aquatic insects, although some insects are omnivorous, eating vegetation as well as other insects.

The food chain involves even the most microscopic organisms. Algae, diatoms, bacteria, protozoa, and flagella are the low end of the food chain. They are collectively referred to as plankton and form the food of the higher orders of insects such as mosquito and midge, as well as larva and pupa. These, in turn, with other forms of plankton are eaten by larger insects such as shrimp, damsel nymph, dragon fly nymph, and mayfly nymph, among others.

Fish feed on all that are large enough to be suitable diet. Trout newly hatched from the egg are not able to handle large food, so depend on plankton during the early part of life. As their size increases they take increasingly larger insects.

Since lakes can have widely varied ecological features, insect life can be equally varied. Some insects, for instance, are particularly adapted to certain types of vegetation, while others favor mud, rocky or marl bottom waters. As can be realized, each lake is inhabited largely by the insects best suited to the particular environment. This last statement, however, causes confusion to many anglers and has resulted in a question I am often asked: "Why do I take fish on a shrimp fly when there are no shrimp in the lake I fish?"

This question applies not only to shrimp but also to many insects. The answer is our hatchery program. On a number of streams there are egg collection stations where eggs are taken for incubating and rearing in a hatchery. When the fry are a suitable size, they are distributed to many lakes in the region.

Fish hatched from eggs taken from one lake and stocked in another in the area are no doubt instinctively familiar with a wide variety of natural insects. Whether or not the insects exist in the lake the fish now inhabits has no bearing on instinctive recognition.

The imitation insect presented at the time of natural emergence, whether or not that insect is present in the water fished, will frequently produce. By contrast, if a hatch of insects peculiar to that body of water is in progress it is not likely to do well.

All aquatic insects, however, inhabit inland waters in various population densities. Lakes particularly suited to sedgeflies, or *chironamidae*, for example, might also have lesser numbers of other insects.

Whether we refer to fish, insects or cows, the principles of pasture remain the same. The environment can only support so much life per acre. The potential of a lake is calculated in pounds of fish per acre because fish is what we are primarily interested in. Were we interested in the production of insect life (and we should be for obvious reasons) productivity also would be recorded in pounds per acre.

Lakes, as with farm pasture, vary widely in their volume of food potential. Although shallow lakes with much algae are among the highest producers, they are not among the most beautiful when the algae bloom. But to the fisherman they can offer superb fishing. The soupy appearance is not detrimental to the fish but produces an abundance of food. Lakes with very clear water may be most attractive to the eye, but to the knowledgeable fisherman it is immediately apparent that there may be few pounds of fish per acre.

The feeding habits of fish are also governed by the fact that every insect order has a time of year for a particular activity, whether it is emergence or seasonal migration to or from deep water. Emergence is the time when nymphs and pupae rise to the surface and become terrestrial in order to mate, lay eggs and start a new cycle of life. Migration is the result of seasonal changes that affect insects which spend more than a year in the developing stage. Nymphs that spend the summer in shoreline weeds and on shallow shoals must move to deeper water before freeze-up or perish in the ice of winter. As spring comes and the ice goes they again take up residence on the shoals and shoreline vegetation. Dropping water levels in summer will also prompt a minor migration to water of a more suitable depth.

Cycles of insect density are also of great importance to the angler as they affect the feeding habits of fish. Ardent fishermen well know that a pattern which is very successful one year will often have disappointing results the following season.

Insect life is prone to fluctuate in population cycles as are the lemming, rabbit, salmon and many other forms of wildlife. These cycles, known as dominant and sub-dominant, are important. A fisherman who is knowledgeable about insects will avoid those waters where the dominant insect population is at a low cycle.

Insect emergence is also affected by lake elevation because of the shorter season at higher levels. In the mountains of the West, lakes up to the 3,000-foot elevation are usually ice free from about the first week of May. From 3,000 to about 4,000 feet, the third week in May is the average opening. Above 4,000 feet it is not wise to make plans for fishing before June first.

Freeze-up is also earlier at the higher elevations, making a season that is from four to six weeks shorter than for lower elevations.

Hatches that occur when the ice first comes off can be followed from lake to lake as elevation increases. This tactic, however, is successful only to a point. Because of the short season at higher elevations, there comes a time when altitudes are equal. Then, since the fall season approaches more quickly at higher elevations, one must work down again to the lower lakes.

When insects are no longer around but lakes are still ice free, there is still excellent fishing for the more hardy anglers. This is the time the fish feed on shrimp, leech and other migrating insects, which usually move quite rapidly as they progress from one hiding place to another on their way to deeper water. The feeding fish intercept these insects by cruising over an area in schools, the size of which to some extent depends on the size of the fish. The larger fish take over the choice waters, leaving smaller fish to follow behind or look for other feeding places.

To fishermen this feeding pattern is far more important than it first appears.

The natural movement of the insects must be considered in terms of direction as well as speed. In the fall it is wise to fish the imitation from shallow to deep water, for fish are extremely sensitive to the smallest details. Size, speed, color and direction of movement of the imitation must closely resemble natural food if trout are to be deceived consistently.

The cruising habits of fish can also be used to advantage if they can be located. Finding them is not always difficult, particularly if there are others fishing the area. Often the person in the boat next to you will take a fish or two, then perhaps you have action for a short time. Then the fisherman to the other side of you seems successful. It is fairly certain there is a school of fish cruising that area for, as they go by, each angler gets some action from it. With a little calculating you are now in a position to move with them provided you do not interfere with the other fishermen. If you cannot move you may be better to stay where you are and wait for their return. Casting to the direction from which the school should come will give you a longer play as you can fish them to the other side of the boat before they are out of reach.

If no other anglers are present and the action ceases, move to one side a short distance. If there is still no action move the other way a greater distance from your original position.

In the early spring the same rules apply except that insect life is moving in the opposite direction — from deep to shallow water — and imitations should be worked accordingly.

In the summer when hatches are occurring fish are not so prone to cruise. They tend to mill in the same general area, particularly when the emergent insect is not the type that clambers out of the water with the aid of vegetation protruding from the water surface. The insect forms that emerge on the water surface usually move more or less directly from the bottom to the surface. Often these hatches will occur in fairly localized areas. Here the fish will mill about, taking the insect as it rises from the bottom. Again the larger fish dominate the choice water, leaving what is left for the smaller fish. Since fish prefer a fairly low light level which is found in the greater depths, this is the place to look for the larger specimens.

The rainbow, or Kamloops, trout is not naturally cannibalistic towards its own young. Under certain conditions, though, cannibalism does occur, particularly in virgin lakes that have recently been stocked. These previously barren lakes have an abundance of insect life and the first fish stocked will grow rapidly. Subsequent stockings, whether natural or otherwise, find the feed less plentiful and grow more slowly. Remnants of the first planting often have a hard time finding enough food to sustain the large body weight and become quite thin. Since the competition is greater with every stocking, the remaining original fish may turn cannibal to support their large size. A cannibal fish will often reveal its feeding location by its method of catching the smaller fish.

Often in the evening a predator trout will cruise the shore line and shoals looking for a school of small fish. When they are located it charges through the school, slashing and striking in all directions. It then comes back, picking up the crippled, stunned and injured.

In shallow water where small fish gather close to the shore, a sudden aerial shower of these little fish is a good indication of predator action, the small ones taking to the air to avoid the ferocious attack.

A fly tied to represent a small trout, dropped among the showering fish and twitched to imitate an injured minnow works well. I once took a 4-pound trout with a 6-inch trout in its stomach.

In lakes where many species of fish are found large trout will frequently feed on small fish but seem to avoid eating their own kind.

Gnat—Larvae
Family—CHIRONOMUS   Order—DIPTERA

This family of insects is large and, because of its widespread occurrence, volume of hatches, tolerance to pollution and range of size is probably the most important. In all stages of development they are food for a large number of invertebrates, so are directly and indirectly of great importance to many varieties of fish species.

The young larvae are microscopic and worm-like, with a many segmented body with what appears to be stubby legs on the first and last body segments. As they mature, before pupation they can reach a size, depending on species, from one-quarter inch to slightly over one inch.

They build larval cases, usually of mud or a jelly-like substance, with the larvae very active. As the time for pupation approaches the case is sealed at the end and the pupae begin development. The food from which they sustain life is algae and decaying vegetable matter. Since this food is found in all bodies of water it is responsible for the larvae's wide occurrence.

The larvae also may be present in very deep water owing to its natural tolerance for low oxygen. They will leave the tube of mud or jelly if disturbed, when growth demands less confining quarters, or when a suitable feeding area is desired. Since the tube is not portable, at every move a new one is made.

These larvae are commonly referred to as blood worms, owing to their

Lakes vary widely in the poundage of fish they produce. This Rocky Mountain lake, while clear and beautiful, wouldn't yield as many fish per acre as a warmer lake in the Kamloops and Nicola Valley rangeland.

bright red coloring. This coloring, however, is not consistent in all species, green and tan being also very common.

The larval state is used as food by many fish and invertebrates of varying species and sizes. I have found from examining stomach contents over a period of years that trout feed on them largely in summer and fall. This feeding pattern doesn't mean that they are not desirable at all times but rather not so available.

There are many commercial flies that are successful imitators, the most useful have thin red bodies on hooks about a size #8 or smaller. The Red Quill, Carey Red, Partridge and Red, and many others have proved useful.

A welcome aspect of this fly is that it is not too critical as to presentation. A wide range of depth and speed may be used, but fishing with a sinking line with a moderately slow retrieve works well. Experimentation is needed to find what is most suitable at any given time.

Gnat—Pupae
Family—CHIRONOMUS   Order—DIPTERA

To the fly angler the pupa is the most important stage in the development of this species. Early in the season stomach contents reveal the large quantities of pupae consumed by fish. Many invertebrates also feed on them during this stage. Hatches of the various species occur during the entire summer and well into fall.

The pupal stage ranges in size from one-quarter inch to over one inch with a very slim body which tapers to the abdominal tip. The head is quite large and the embryonic legs and wings, called prolegs, are in the form of fleshy appendages directly behind and underneath the head. At the front of the head is a plumose structure, the function of which is debatable as authorities vary in their opinions. To the fisherman it is of little consequence. The main thing to know is that it does exist and is of importance in imitations.

It is questionable whether or not the pupae partake of food. In the pupal stage of short duration, there may be little, if any, need of sustenance. To the average angler, however, it really doesn't matter if the pupae eat or not.

Since larvae live both in deep and more shallow waters, the pupation takes place at all depths. The pupa emerging from the case, or tube, rises directly to the surface in a vertical migratory path.

The method of propulsion is a rapid undulation of the body, rest and repeat, until it reaches the surface. Here it may rest for a short time, its head at the water surface and body at a slight angle. After a short time the head splits open and a tiny mosquito-like fly emerges.

Pupal coloration varies with species. Most common are black and light green, although dark green, brown and tan are also important colors. On all species the plumose structure on the front of the head is white and prominent, a feature not to be overlooked on imitations.

Fish feeding on these pupae do so in a rather lazy manner. There is no need to hurry since the pupae move rather slowly and hatch in great abundance. An imitation taken by a fish can be mouthed and spit out easily and quickly without ever the slightest signal to the angler. Fish feeding on these pupae at or near the water surface are often thought to be taking the emerged adult fly. In reality they come up over the top and take the pupae on the way down, ignoring any or all terrestrial adults on the surface.

There are very few good imitations commercially available. It may be better to use an easily acquired pattern that has the required body characteristics, and with small scissors trim to the desired appearance.

Patterns of this nature include dry fly mosquito and black and green bivisible patterns. Among wet flies are a thin bodied Doc Spratley (remove wings) or brown quill (remove hackle). There are, you will find, many other patterns that can be doctored in a like manner.

The gnat is a productive imitation although difficult to fish. The method in which the fish takes the fly is responsible for a great many missed fish. The vertical movement of the natural pupa — and the fish is extremely critical of any variation in this movement — with its slow progress to the surface and the delicate acceptance by the fish make it the most interesting of all imitators. But once the angler learns the subtleties of presenting his imitation all the frustration and failures will be forgotten.

In shallow water a floating line is most valuable. The sudden movement of the 6 inches of line adjoining the leader is the clue to a strike, if it in truth can be called a strike. In deep water a sinking line is the most valuable. Here the clue is where the line enters the water. At a very slight unnatural movement strike immediately or you miss the fish.

Gnat—Terrestrial

Family—CHIRONOMUS   Order—DIPTERA

In the adult terrestrial stage this insect is not of great importance as a fish food, the bulk of these insects being taken in the pupal form. Smaller fish in shallow water take most, as much in a spirit of play as to secure food, and both terrestrial dragon flies and damsel flies feed on them.

The species range in length from three-sixteenths of an inch to five-eighths inch with a moderately thin body tapering to the tip of the abdomen. The thorax is quite heavy, the wings emerging from there are shorter than the body and held parallel to it when at rest. The head is small and well defined with a broad brush-like antenna. Legs are long and when at rest on the water surface are held well spread with the rear ones at a 45-degree angle from and nearly as long as the body.

Whether or not they feed at this stage I do not know. However, they do not bite as mosquitoes are prone to do, though large hatches can be almost as annoying, flying into eyes, nose and ears with accompanying discomfort. When good hatches occur they fly over the water in dense clouds, usually from late morning to mid afternoon.

Many of these insects are black bodied, with greens and coppery browns less common. The abdominal segment lines are paler than the body in the green and brown variation, while the black-bodied insects have white or grey segment lines.

As the adult emerges from the pupal case the wings are cinnamon brown, quickly turning a light grey as they dry. The insect then takes to the air, frequently landing on and taking off from the water surface.

Some of these flies are taken by trout while at rest on the surface. Often the smaller fish combine play and feeding in one operation, thus are attracted to the adult gnat. The larger fish prefer the pupae as they rise to the surface before emergence.

Imitations of this fly are readily available at most sporting goods stores under a variety of names. The mosquito, variant and bivisible patterns and many others may be used. These are all dry fly patterns and should be made to float well.

The dry, or floating, line is the only one that can be used with success. As the natural insect moves little on the water but lands on and takes directly off the surface a retrieve is not required. Just enough movement to agitate the water about the fly is sufficient to attract the attention of any fish that may be close by.

Water Boatman
Order—CORIXA

A seasonally important insect, the water boatman is found in all ponds and lakes that have even small amounts of weed on the bottom.

One would think the water boatman, being active through the entire season, could be expected to be found at least occasionally in the stomach contents of fish throughout the season. Surprisingly, however, very early spring and late fall are the only times this insect appears in the fish's diet.

An air breathing insect, the water boatman must come to the surface at intervals to replenish air supply which is trapped in the form of a bubble on the underside of its body. As the insect swims to the weeds on the lake bottom, the bubble reflects light and shows a slightly greenish or yellow silver flash as the insect turns, swimming erratically down. Once on the bottom it must cling to sticks or weeds, otherwise it would float to the surface.

This small beetle-like insect feeds on decaying vegetation and the remains of dead insects. It is about one-quarter to three-eighths inch long and one-eighth inch or slightly over in width with a broad head and a body bluntly tapering to the tip of the abdomen. Directly behind the head on the underside are three pairs of legs. The forward two pairs are for grasping and climbing. The rear pair, at right angles to the body, are used only for swimming, the action much the same as oars in a boat — hence the name water boatman.

About the time of the first autumn frost the water boatman take off on their nuptial flight. Aided by the wind, they travel great distances, not infrequently landing on glistening wet pavement in huge numbers. They will also land on frozen lakes where they seem unable to become airborne again and may be found frozen in the ice in the spring. I have, at times, thawed them out and they seem to suffer little from the experience.

The back of these insects is a solid rich brown, the underside a pale watery green or pale yellow. In the water this underside is covered with the air bubble, giving a silvery luster to its color.

As soon as the lakes are ice free these insects appear, although not in great abundance. As very few other insects are about and the fish are tired of a winter's diet of shrimp, they are for a few weeks taken readily by the foraging trout. For reasons I have never been able to fathom, trout do not take them again until the first autumn frosts. Then, preparing for their nuptial flights, the water boatman leave and enter the water on sunny days from late morning until mid afternoon.

To catch the trout, there is an English fly pattern called "Corixa." To my knowledge it is the only one ever attempted commercially, but is seldom seen on this side of the Atlantic. There are a number of flies, however, that with minor changes can be used and are commercially available.

These include the brown Carey, on a #10 hook; a reddish brown Tom Thumb with the tail cut off and fished as a wet fly; also the Brown Hackle with most of the hackle removed. Success is often achieved by fishing with a fast sinking line of #2 density.

These insects have a fairly rapid progress and the imitation must be fished quite fast with a fairly long retrieve in order to best represent a natural. Size and movement seem more critical than color. Drab browns of many shades, small in size with rather plump bodies, are the best imitations.

Midge—Larvae
Family—CHAOBORUS

These insects are such an important part of the fish's diet that it will feed on them to the exclusion of all else at frequent times during spring and early summer. The midge is widespread, found in virtually all lake and pond waters. It is a related species to the mosquito without the blood-sucking tendencies so annoying to man.

It is one-half inch long with a very slim body, having a head with a prominent eye and a proboscis that appears to come from the upper part of the head and curve down over the mouth. Behind the head is a definite hump, followed by a slightly upward curving body, ending in a long taper. On the underside of tail and body is a brush-like appendage presumably used for propulsion — a rapid doubling and straightening movement. Progress is rapid but sporadic. At rest it lies in a horizontal position and can remain unmoving at any depth.

Midge frequent open water and shoreline weeds, feeding on microscopic organisms. They are very hardy. Even when removed from the stomach of fish and put into water they immediately become active. In addition to fish, shrimp and many other insects feed on them.

In the larval stage these insects are referred to as glass worms owing to the transparent characteristics of the body, the only coloration a small spot near the head and another close to the tail. On occasion the visible digestive tract will have a red, green or yellow coloration showing as a thin line. The color depends on the food ingested, although it is never enough to affect the overall translucence to any appreciable degree.

There are no commercially available patterns representing this stage of the insect's development. Although those tied by individual fly fishermen meet with little success, very thin tinsel bodies and sparse pale yellow hackle are the most effective. They are fished with a dry line, the fly allowed to sink and then given an occasional twitch to simulate the sporadic movement.

Midge—Pupae
Family—CHAOBORUS

The pupal form of this insect is equal in importance to the larval stage, forming a large part of the diet of many species of insects and fish.

The transition from larva to pupa takes place without the protection of a case, or tube, as is common with many other orders of insects. The small pupa, three sixteenths to five sixteenths of an inch long, maintains a vertical position in the water. The shape is that of a comma. The head is quite large, the bulbous portion forward of the body and the eyes situated on the forward extremity. At the upper part of the head is what appears to be two ears held erect, giving the insect a rather alert, intelligent appearance. The body, which curves downward and slightly forward, is visibly segmented, tapering abruptly to a very short fibre-like tail.

The pupa moves by a rapid forward and up, downward and back, movement of the lower portion of its body as it moves to the water surface to emerge into a mosquito-like fly. Color ranges from a dark green, brown and tan to greenish yellow.

The fish feed on this insect at all depths, with even large trout finding it desirable owing to its abundance. However, I do not know of any commercial imitations of this insect form.

Some fly fishermen have developed very successful patterns, usually tied on #16 hooks or smaller, bodies brown or tan with darker heads. Very small mosquito dry flies in the proper colors also can be converted to reasonable imitations by cutting off the wings and hackle, leaving just enough to form a large head.

Suitable lines to fish these flies are the dry line, sinking tip and slow sinker #1.

There is no strike in the true sense but rather a gentle sucking in. If the slight unnatural movement of the line is not detected in time to strike the fish, the fly is frequently spit out and a fish lost. This type of fishing requires concentration and some practice. Owing to the small size of the fly, very fine leaders are required or they cannot be threaded through the eye of the hook. For this reason the most delicate use of the rod is of paramount importance, otherwise the fly may be broken off.

Midge—Terrestrial
Family—CHAOBORUS

The terrestrial form of this insect is so similar to that of the great gnat family (*chironomus*) that only an expert on dipterous orders can offer positive identification.

All information as to size and importance as a fish and insect food is so similar to that of the gnat as to make further reference repetitious. Color is one of the widest differences — grey, green and amber being the most dominant.

For the dry fly imitator, this order can be treated as a mosquito pattern so common in all sporting goods stores.

Mayfly—Nymph
Family—EPHEMEROPTERA

Mayfly nymphs form a large part of the diet of many aquatic insects and fish of various species. A large order of insects, mayflies inhabit all fresh water both in streams and ponds, in every part of the world. It is not possible to describe them in any detail but rather in a general way. Of the numerous mayfly species, many are found only in flowing waters, while others are restricted to still waters by nature of their physical structure and food requirements.

Sensitive to the effects of pollution, they have been virtually eliminated from many waters where they were once seen in dense clouds in mid afternoon and early evening from May to August.

The oil from outboard motors has contributed greatly to their decline. On small lakes where motors can in a few hours deposit sufficient oil to form a film through which the nymph is unable to emerge, it soon dies, breaking the reproduction chain. This loss of individuals in a large number of insect orders greatly reduces the food potential, accounting for a decline in fish population in a great number of lakes.

The many kinds of mayfly nymphs found in lakes vary in size from one-eighth inch to one inch in length. The head is well defined and distinct from the body, which is long and tapering to the abdominal tip, from which protrudes three tails. At rest the body is curved slightly upward, the long tails also curving upward at the basal section with a slight reversing at the outward tip. An embryo wing case is very distinct over what might be termed the shoulders. In color, mayfly nymphs are pale yellow, tan, light mottled brown, grey, pale green and black.

Seven pairs of gills, found along the abdomen in the form of paddle-like appendages, vary in size, form and placement depending on the species and contribute much to the overall appearance of the insect. Six legs, reasonably long and strong, are used for clambering among the sticks and vegetation on the lake bottom. When swimming, mayflies with a large gill structure move rapidly by an up and down undulation of the abdomen, while those with a smaller gill structure appear to dart a short distance by rapid body movement, rest and again dart a short way.

Many species spend more than a year in the nymphal state. As time for emergence approaches the wing case becomes quite large and very dark in color. Shortly thereafter the insect emerges into the first terrestrial stage called a "dun."

Where, except in B.C., can a fly fisherman be visited by a curious caribou? The rainy-day lake is Clearwater in Wells Gray Park.

As with many insect orders, when time for emergence approaches the mayfly becomes restless, moving about impatiently with frequent false starts to the surface. This nervous activity precedes emergence by as much as a week in many orders of insects. At these times the nymphs become more obvious to the fish and are eaten in large numbers before the terrestrials are seen on the surface. For this reason it is important to the fly fisherman to know the average emergence dates of the various insect orders in the lakes he frequents so that he can take advantage of this characteristic.

The widespread occurrence and large numbers of species in this order is no doubt responsible for the large number of fly patterns designed to imitate the different stages of mayfly development. Standard patterns that are well known and commonly available are too numerous to mention. A few of the main popular ones are the Blue Dun nymph, Hares Ear nymph, Half Back, and Hendrickson nymph. In appearance the imitators accent the large wing case, the long tails and gill structure. Color varies so widely even on the so-called "standard patterns" as to be unworthy of discussion.

Fishing this imitation is dependent to a large extent on what is occurring — pre-hatch activity, rising to the surface, or surface emergence. Although this surface emergence is normal under most weather conditions, some conditions cause an emerging prior to reaching the water surface. At these times the insect leaves the nymphal skin a short distance below and rises in a bubble of air. At these times the fly is seen to "pop" to the surface.

Sinking lines, sinking tip and dry lines are all used to advantage, depending on the nymphal activity one wishes to simulate. Simulating pre-hatch activity requires a sinking line about #2 density and a slow retrieve. Sometimes this retrieve is short and hesitant, at others more continuous, depending on the species present.

The sinking tip line is used when fishing more shallow water, or when

46

the nymphs are rising to the surface. This line gives a natural lift to the imitator, the effect of which is measured in terms of success.

When the nymphs hatch well below the surface and the fly "pops" to the top of the water, a sinking tip is also used. A dry fly is used to simulate the emerging dun, the sinking portion of the line allowed to go below the surface until it pulls the fly under. Now retrieve at a moderate speed. As the fly starts to rise from a foot or two below the water surface it assumes the appearance of a natural.

When nymphs emerge normally at the surface and fish activity indicates they are feeding on nymphs rather than dry flies, a dry line is used to fish the imitation just under the surface.

Fish at this time rise in a very low arc, head or tail seldom seen. At other times large fish will barely dimple the water as they suck the nymphs from just under the surface tension. A strike will rarely be experienced at these times and the line must be watched closely where it joins the leader to detect the slightest movement as a fish takes the offering. Hesitating to strike when this movement occurs loses fish since they spit the fly out very quickly on discovering their error.

Mayfly—Terrestrial
Family—EPHEMEROPTERA

The mayfly is one of the few terrestrial forms that is of great significance in the diet of fish of all sizes. Large fish take these flies readily, expending considerable energy while feeding on them. This characteristic attests to the desirability of these insects as food. Large fish, like large people, are often loath to expend more than the minimal amount of energy required to accomplish the desired results. Nevertheless, few insects in the winged form attract large fish in lakes and ponds to the extent that a good hatch of mayflies will. The large number of species and the appetite fish have for this fly accounts for the vast number of commercial dry fly patterns which imitate it.

As already mentioned, the mayfly as it leaves the nymphal case is called a dun. It has yet to shed another skin before it reaches the final reproduction stage known to fly fishermen as "spinners."

The duns, as they emerge in numbers from the nymphal skin and rest on the water, appear as a flotilla of tiny sail boats drifting over the water in a light breeze. In the late morning and early evening they are often the target for many rising fish.

Shortly after emerging the duns leave the water and fly to nearby shelter, usually weeds or trees where the transition from dun to spinner is accomplished by shedding the outer skin. Except for a rather startling color change, the fly is now much as it was prior to molting.

The fly as a dun is a dark-colored insect, usually about three-eighths to one-half inch long exclusive of the tails which are as long as the body. Two or four wings (depending on species) held upright and tight together arise from a rather prominent upper thorax. The delicate tapered body has a long upward curve to the abdomen tip where two or three long tails are at times held almost erect and well spread when at rest. Color is drab — solid and mottled greys, browns and green.

Other than color, the spinner undergoes no visible physical change from the dun. Wings become transparent or white, sometimes with a slight mottling. The body can be several colors — yellow, tan, pale green, brown, grey, bronze and black — each peculiar to the species.

To the fly angler the terrestrial mayfly is the most important dry fly of summer. Although some species hatch early in May, various others frequently appear at intervals as late as September. Fly patterns of this insect stage are numerous and easily obtained at most retail fishing shops. The March Brown, Blue Dun, August Dun, Iron Blue Dun, Olive Dun and many more offer the fisherman a wide choice.

The floating line is the only one that has any value for the proper presentation of dry fly versions of this terrestrial. Light leaders, soft at the tip, are preferred to allow a natural unrestricted appearance to the fish. Leaders that are stiff or overly large in diameter tend to roll the fly or will not permit a natural rise and fall as the fly rests on the lightly wind-riffled surface. Big fish are smart and every detail is important when trying to outwit them!

Fish rising to a dry fly will be seen breaking the water in a tight little arc but will at no time be completely clear of the water. Fish rising in this manner do not take the fly on the way up but come over the top and take it on the way down. This is the reason for so many missed fish. The fisherman is inclined to strike immediately the fish breaks the water, thereby pulling the fly away before the fish has taken it.

On rather cold days early in the season duns seem reluctant to leave the water surface. Fish then simply come underneath and suck them down, much as they do when taking nymphs immediately under the surface.

A retrieve designed to impart a lifelike movement over the water is not natural. Any slight breeze will accomplish a natural drift far more effectively than any movement the angler can impart, provided the fly is presented at a proper angle to the wind direction. If the naturals are drifting with the wind and the cast is made downwind, the imitation will either stay relatively still or, when retrieved, travel in a direction opposite to the drift of the naturals. Only the most stupid fish would be fooled in this situation. Utilize the wind for a natural drift and just twitch the line occasionally to impart a restless sort of movement as if the fly were saying, "Well, I'm going to take off now."

The best advice I can offer is to watch what the fish and the insects are doing. Then ask yourself if there is a pattern to the feeding movement or a concentration of activity in one area. Often during an offshore wind fish will lie in the breakoff where a shoal suddenly dips to deep water. Here they will wait for the wind to drift the flies over them.

Damselfly—Nymph

Order—ODONATA Sub-Order—ZYGOPTERA

This large important order of aquatic insects contains many species, some of which are peculiar to streams, while others favor still waters.

This insect has a life span of up to three years in the nymphal state and a varied appearance in the numerous stages of growth. At each stage the nymph sheds its old skin and in a short time a new one is formed by the new outer surface toughening. This stage, between molts, is called an "instar."

It is important to the fisherman to note that immediately after the old skin is cast the insect is a pale watery green or yellowy green, becoming darker over the next few days. Immediately after the molt the insect is shy, hiding under vegetation or whatever is available. At this stage of development it seems to know what a tender delicacy it is for other insects and many species of fish.

In the early stages of growth it is mostly inactive. Even though it has the ability to move freely, it chooses to stay in one place for long periods of time, usually in the foliage of bottom growth where it waylays the smaller insects on which it feeds.

Its head is large, flat and broad with a bulbous eye, high on either side. The thorax is quite heavy, on the upper side of which the embryo wing case begins to form early in the insect's development. From the underside six legs of moderate length give mobility in the weeds. The abdomen is long and very slender, while the tail has much the appearance of the tail surfaces of an aircraft with three large paddle-like appendages. One is held almost vertical from the central axis of the body, the lower two continuing on the same axis but angled left and right from it.

These insects are slow active swimmers during spring and fall migration. When freeing themselves from the nymphal skin they usually swim to the shallow water close to the shore. They swim with legs extended at right angles to their body, moving their abdomen vigorously from side to side while making slow progress toward shore. When a suitable support is reached they crawl to a height that will be safe from the now dangerous waves. Here they fasten their feet firmly and emergence begins. The new insect now bears no resemblance to its earlier form.

Newly hatched from the egg, it is microscopic in size and translucent. As further development takes place its body becomes colored, darkening through the numerous instars until immediately prior to emergence. Although olive green and tan mottled with brown are most commonly seen, water color, bottom fauna and food ingested affect color, sometimes to a remarkable degree. Clear water and green weed bottom produce nymphs of various shades of green. Algae water, with its yellow-green influence, gives them a pale watery yellow to brownish tan. Specimens that have been feeding on any of the red organisms take on a bright red or deep maroon, depending on the feed involved.

To the fly fisherman this insect is of great importance. It appears as early as late May in the low elevation lakes, often remaining to mid-September. The average for most areas is from June to September. Here, again, the pre-emergence activity that occurs as much as a week before the first terrestrial damselflies are seen is an important factor.

Sinking tip and floating lines are the most useful, occasionally sinking lines of #2 density prove very successful, particularly in clear water.

Most often these nymphs are seen to swim to within a short distance of the surface, well out from the shore. Then they proceed to the shoreline weeds, swimming only a few feet to a few inches under the surface. Progress is slow with frequent rests. If disturbed they will immediately swim sluggishly to the bottom.

Line retrieve must be made to imitate the insect's progress. I have successfully used a slow 12- to 14-inch line recovery, pausing every three or four pulls for as much as 30 seconds, repeating until reaching the leader. The strike is frequently as gentle as a puff of wind moving the line; at other times as vicious as a snapping dog.

Many commercial fly patterns, called "damsel nymph," lack so much in the way of imagination as to be ridiculous. The best imitation I have seen that requires little trimming is an English pattern called the "Greenwell Glory nymph." This fly is a good representation but can be improved by trimming the hackle at top and bottom, leaving the sides intact.

A muddy tan or pale green body, long and thin with a rather short bushy tail, is required to best imitate this insect. I am sure the imaginative fly fisherman will have no difficulty finding patterns that can be trimmed to meet these requirements, even if he does not dress his own flies.

Damselfly—Terrestrial
Order—ODONATA   Sub-Order—ZYGOPTERA

The winged stage of the damselfly is not of great importance to the fly fisherman. Fish do not seem to relish these insects as part of their diet. While in years past I have had good days with the fly it is not, however, one that I consider indispensable.

During times of good hatches these flies will be seen clinging to rushes close to the shore and on shallow shoals, looking much like blue flowers resting on stems and lily pads. Sometimes they hover a few inches above the water in such vast numbers that from a distance they appear as a blue mist.

Fish feeding on these insects hit the rushes on which the fly rests, knocking many to the water then leisurely returning to devour the soggy unfortunate victims. Variations of the same technique are used when these flies are at rest on small logs and lily pads.

This fly has a large head and thick thorax from which two pairs of wings emerge to lie parallel to the body when at rest. Its six legs are short in comparison to the body, strong and used for grasping weeds and branches on which they rest. In flight the legs are held basket-like and are used to catch and hold the smaller flies on which they feed while flying. Its two pairs of transparent wings are long and narrow, broadening to the outward tip, with a single small black spot close to the leading edge of each tip. The body is extremely long and thin, the reason these flies are often referred to as "blue darning needles."

Copulation is accomplished in the air. The flies are often seen flying in pairs and are the coupled bluettes we hear about. Eggs are laid directly on the water or deposited on the bottom by climbing down a weed stem to the desired location. The method depends on the species involved.

The damselfly commonly seen in most areas is a brilliant blue, banded with black, or a muddy light brown also banded with black. I suspect these are different phases of the same species. They are often seen coupled while flying low over the water on a summer afternoon. Some species are red and others green, but they do not have the wide distribution that the blue damselfly has.

A floating line best presents imitations of this terrestrial insect. Fish close to the sedge grass and rushes, presenting the fly as to represent insects fallen to the water. Let the floating imitation lie for a moment, twitching it occasionally to represent a struggling insect. Usually on windy days the insects that are emerging on the weeds will fall to the water before development and drying of their wings is complete. Color at this time is not fully developed, being usually a pale muddy yellow or olive dun. These soft immature flies, however, are often more palatable to the fish than the fully terrestrial insect.

Commercially available patterns that are reasonably close to the mature terrestrial stage in appearance are the Nations Blue Dragon, Teal and Blue, and Teal and Silver. Patterns used for the immature terrestrial — the Yellow Carey, Invicta and Queen of the Waters — have proven successful.

Dragonfly—Nymph
Order—ODONATA   Sub-Order—ANISOPTERA

The dragonfly is well known and includes a large number of species. Some are peculiar to streams while others favor the still waters of lakes, ponds and swamps. In the terrestrial state a wide range of colors and sizes are seen flying and darting swiftly over the water.

The nymphs of these species are not so well known but are most important insects in the diet of various fish. The period of nymphal development from the egg through many instars to the terrestrial emergence is up to 4 years in some species. They therefore provide food for this length of time compared to a few days in the terrestrial form.

These nymphs have the ability to move freely and rapidly, but are more inclined to stalk their prey by moving very slowly and cautiously through the weeds. They often lie in wait under logs and rocks close to the shore where they feed on shrimp, mayfly nymphs and even very small fish.

Their rapid movement is accomplished by taking in water through the posterior orifice, then expelling it in a jet stream that propels the insect forward some 4 to 6 inches. By repeating this process they cover a considerable distance in a relatively short time.

Specimens have attained two inches, although the average just before emergence is about one and one-half inches. Its head is very broad and quite flat across the front with a large eye on either side. Technical details of the mouth parts will be dispensed with as they are of little importance to the fisherman, other than for species identification.

The thorax is deep and quite narrow, on the top of which in the more advanced stages of growth embryo wings are easily recognized. On the underside of the thorax are six strong, thick legs. The front pair are quite short while the following two pair are progressively longer, the hindmost pair reaching to the rear of the body.

The abdomen, narrow at the thorax, gradually widens until maximum at about four-fifths of the insect's total length. From this point it quickly tapers to a short, tail-like, segmented appendage surrounding the vent. In cross section the body is roughly triangular, flat on the underside, sloping uppersides, rounded over the top. The abdomen is noticeably segmented.

The youngest nymphs (three-eighths inch) important to the fly fisherman are dark green or black with noticeable pale green segmentation, the thorax showing as a wide pale watery green where the wing case will eventually form. As development progresses the dark green modifies to a light muddy olive, the pale green portions darkening until the entire insect is a muddy olive green. As maturing continues, dark brown to black markings appear on the back in the form of broken stripes. The embryo wing case is now becoming quite evident. Another nymph with similar body form but smaller is black through the entire development.

Water and lake bottom environment influences color in these nymphs to a marked degree. In lakes with a dark bottom caused by muck or much-decayed vegetation, or water the color of weak coffee, the nymphs will be a brownish olive green with black markings. Immediately after molting these nymphs are a pale translucent green with very large black prominent eyes. As the exoskeleton hardens it gradually becomes darker and in about a week the former color reappears.

Fish feed on these nymphs at all seasons, including their spring migration to shallow water, their search for a suitable support above water where transformation to terrestrial occurs and their fall migration from shallow to deep water. The size of these insects through their various growth stages is important to fly anglers, particularly in the latter part of the season. Since the large nymphs in the emergent year of development are gone and next year's crop is not fully developed, anglers must fish smaller imitations in the fall than in the early season.

This nymph is well represented by a large number of commercially available flies in a wide range of sizes. The Doc Spratley in black, brown, yellow and shades of green and the Carey type dressed in the same colors are the most useful with and without tinsel ribbing. Flies that are dressed with a silver ribbing should be used in the early part of the season, while a gold ribbing is better in the late season. The reason is changing light conditions, explained in the chapter on light.

Floating, sinking tip and sinking lines are all used to advantage, depending on circumstances such as depth of water, time of year and type of bottom.

The migrating nymph — moving in short jet-like spurts — starts quickly, gradually slows then again starts quickly. While it is not possible to retrieve line in this fashion, the fish is not able to distinguish beginning from end of propulsion. For this reason if the angler retrieves about 10 inches of line slowly, ending with a rather sharp jerk, it well represents the movement of a natural.

The non-migrating nymph moves entirely differently. It slowly crawls over and through the weeds, sticks or rocks, occasionally darting a short distance, then lying still for long periods. This action is best duplicated with a sinking tip line, a very short slow retrieve with frequent brief pauses, then a long pull. With this method, the floating portion of the line lifts the imitation clear of the weeds to make rapid progess for a short distance, then settle and again move slowly over the bottom.

The fast-moving fly is often struck hard and firmly while the slow-moving imitation frequently seems to hang slightly as if it hooked a weed. It is not necessary to strike the fish hard but rather to immediately tighten the line. The response of the fish will set the hook.

Dragonfly—Terrestrial
Order—ODONATA   Sub-Order—ANISOPTERA

The dragonfly is one of the largest terrestrial insects, some species having a wing spread of slightly over 4 inches and a body length of about 3 1/2 inches. Its wings are usually transparent and strongly veined, some species having color in them. The body has bright, almost fluorescent, colors of green, blue, red, yellow and shiny black. Its head is large with huge compound eyes, a short neck fixed to a very heavy thorax from the upper side of which two pair of wings extend at right angles to a long thin body. Legs are of medium length, strong and used for grasping the weed stems and other vegetation on which it rests and for catching smaller insects while feeding on the wing. It is a strong fast flier, hovering and darting around lakes, ponds and marshes during the summer in all parts of the country.

The terrestrial stage of the dragonfly as a trout food is, in my experience, extremely limited. Having over the past 40 years examined the stomach contents of hundreds of fish, on only two occasions have I found these insects. I do not consider it worthwhile, therefore, to imitate this insect form.

Red-shouldered Dragonfly—Nymph
Order—ODONATA   Sub-Order—ANISOPTERA

The nymph of the red-shouldered dragonfly is worthy of separate mention by virtue of different characteristics of importance. While there are undoubtedly a number of species with the same form and habits, I am not familiar with the microscopic details used to place them in their respective niche. I am satisfied to note only those characteristics I feel important to a fly fisherman. Having nurtured members of this family of dragonflies in aquaria many times during the past 15 years and having enjoyed excellent results on imitations of them, I feel the information is worth passing on.

Body form is quite spider-like in appearance. The head is large, angular and flat across the front, with eyes prominent and set high on the outer forward extremity. Its thorax is narrow, legs long and well spread and abdomen almost round-looking from above but angular in cross section, being flat on the underside. This nymph is often as long as three quarters of an inch.

It is shy by nature, hiding mainly in weeds on the lake bottom. It has rather a furry appearance and sometimes has bits of weed and dead vegetation adhering to it. This debris effectively camouflages its location from where its long, arm-like under jaw can grasp passing insects on which it feeds.

When the time approaches to emerge terrestrially it crawls slowly over the bottom to the shore. It may then go quite some distance to climb on rocks or up trees. In fact it is not uncommon to find empty nymphal skins in large numbers on lake-side cabin walls and screens in July.

This nymph is a pale yellow green in the early stages of development, becoming darker as it matures. In mud bottom and dark-water lakes its color is a greenish olive brown, pale to medium in tone. Two dark stripes run the length of its body and extend over the face. Its long legs are barred with the same colors as the body, giving them a mottled appearance.

To fish imitations of this nymph a sinking line or, occasionally, a sinking tip line, is most useful. Work the line slowly, close to the bottom weeds. For this reason it is not an easy fly to use as it frequently hangs in weeds. Since a fish taking the fly has much the same feel, the result is frequent striking when in fact there is no fish there. Frustrating though they are at times, imitations are a good producer.

Many flies can be doctored to imitate this nymph but I know of none tied commercially to represent it. Flies dressed with seal fur bodies are soft, fluffy and rough in appearance, matching this nymph. If the color selection is within reason, and a Carey type hackle tied sparsely, it will work well if properly used.

Shrimp

Order—AMPHIPODA

This small crustacean is probably the most important of all organisms on which trout feed, particularly when hatches of fly larvae, pupae and terrestrials are not present. Abundant populations of shrimp are responsible for the deep pink color of the flesh of Kamloops trout. This coloration in the flesh is always an indication of shrimp. Many of the larger nymphs such as dragonfly and damselfly nymphs also use shrimp as a major part of their diet.

Shrimp, as their development progresses, can be found in sizes from almost microscopic young to three quarters of an inch long, the average being one-half inch.

They have a tough segmented exoskeleton, the body strongly curved over the back to the tail which is short with a slight upward sweep. At the front of the body there are legs used for grasping and holding, to the rear are legs used for climbing, swimming and crawling. Four antennae, or feelers, protrude from the head forward and are from one third to one half the body length.

Shrimp are omnivorous, feeding on small invertebrates, algae and

B.C. hatcheries annually produce up to 6 million rainbow and other fish to stock some 800 lakes. Hatcheries explain why a fish will take a shrimp fly even though there are no natural shrimp in the lake. (See page 35.)

vegetation. Their movements are very erratic, swimming and tumbling through the water, clambering in and around rocks and sticks and through many types of aquatic weeds. At times they can be found only by lifting stones or sticks under which they gather in large numbers.

During copulation they travel in pairs for many days. As the young develop they are carried in a thoric pouch before they leave the parent and become independent.

The color of this crustacean is to a large extent governed by the environment. In algae-type water they are frequently yellow, orange-tan and brown. In clear water they become pale watery green to a rather dark sage green with a slight brown tone on the back. I have also seen specimens bright red, bright blue and an almost fluorescent green. The thoric pouch of the female, owing to the color of the young shrimp therein, is often swollen and yellow in appearance.

Fish are frequently selective when feeding on shrimp. At times only very small ones are attractive; at other times only full grown ones will interest them. They are equally selective as to color, with even the shade at times of extreme importance.

A great many shrimp patterns are available in sporting goods stores in a wide range of colors and sizes. As a fishing consultant in a sporting goods store, I frequently hear someone say: "I have never caught a fish on a shrimp yet!"

I am not in the least surprised. I mentioned earlier that very few commercially available imitators are even reasonable representations of a particular insect. Shrimp lead this category. How any fish, even the most gullible, could possibly accept them for what they are supposed to represent puts considerable strain on the imagination.

Nevertheless, a shrimp fly, well tied and in a variety of colors and sizes, is one of the most productive of patterns. Sizes from a #14 to #8 hook are the most useful. A #10 has proved the best for me. In color, pale yellow, chartreuse, a greyish medium olive and opalescent blue are the most effective.

For shrimp imitations that must be purchased it is well to stay away from the so-called "shrimp patterns." Select instead flies that can be trimmed to a reasonable facsimile. Among these are many of the woolly worm patterns. With the top and side hackle removed and the bottom hackle shortened to the depth of the hook, a more reasonable representation can be attained. Keep in mind the hook size required, as the woolly worm is dressed on rather large hooks.

In the early part of the season lakes with weed-grown shallows should be fished with a dry line, working the fly just above the weeds. Later in the season shrimp move to deeper water where a sinking tip line, or slow sinking #1, becomes most useful. Depending on the water quality of the lake — colored, algae or clear — shrimp can be found at any depth because of the degree of light penetration. Nevertheless, seldom is a line more dense than a fast sinking #2 required to reach the desired depth in a reasonable length of time.

Since shrimp move erratically — up, down, and to either side — one must be careful to avoid any semblance to a rhythmic retrieve, regardless of line used. A moderately slow retrieve with frequent stops and quick short movements interspersed with an occasional long slow recovery of line best imitates the movement of this crustacean.

Leech

Family—HIRUDINEA

The leech is an important invertebrate in the diet of trout and is abundant in most ponds and lakes. Owing to its large size, it is usually found in fish over 12 inches long.

It is available to the fish at all seasons of the year, but spends much time in the mud bottom and on the underside of lily pads and logs. Here it feeds on snails and many dead and decaying organisms from which it extracts the body fluids. On occasion it will attach to turtles and other creatures for a meal of blood, although it can survive for long periods without feeding.

The leech is long and worm-like, capable of remarkable contraction. It may often be seen swimming quite rapidly with an undulating motion, at other times holding a vertical position under the water surface, its body slowly moving in a wave-like motion. It can also be seen in shallow water, its sucker disc attached to some object, the other end swinging and swaying, searching for another hold, or crawling worm-like over the bottom. While some specimens have been reported over 6 inches long, 2 to 4 inches are the most important to fishermen. Most common colors are black, grey and a muddy tan with dark mottling and at times a deep maroon undertone.

The most useful line to fish imitations is the sinking of #2 density, although the sinking tip at infrequent times can be used to advantage.

Water from 15 to 40 feet deep is most productive as fish feed on leech more during midsummer than at other times of the year. The retrieve should be long and of moderate speed. It is most advantageous to stand while fishing this fly as standing allows more freedom of movement. By grasping the line at the rod and letting the hand drop slowly to the side, about 30 inches of line will be recovered at each pull. During times of fair to strong winds when waves are running quite high a faster retrieve is more productive.

Fish are inclined to come from behind a leech and suck it in, creating a problem to many fishermen because of what is termed a "short strike." After a few short strikes they trim the dressing of the fly close to the end of the hook and ruin the fly. Since the fish suck the natural from behind, it moves backward to some extent but the imitation, being fixed to a line, will not and a kind of tug, tug signal is experienced. The tendency is to strike and when the fish is not hooked, retrieve all line and make another cast. This technique is wrong. When this gentle tugging is felt ignore it and continue recovering line at the normal speed. The fish seem to swing away but after a very short time come to the fly either from the side or head on, usually smashing it quite viciously, and frequently being hooked well back in the tongue.

Flies that imitate the leech are the flies of that name and many of the Carey patterns in black, brown and maroon, all with rather long heavy hackle.

Sedgefly—Larvae
Order—TRICHOPTERA

Since this order of insects is a large one, only a few of the most important to fly anglers will be referred to here. All look similar, having a moth-like appearance from the tiniest of flies to those one and one-half inches long. As fish food this species is valuable all through the fishing season in all its stages and development — larva, pupa and terrestrial. For this reason during the midsummer evenings these flies in terrestrial form are responsible for much of the surface activity of trout.

The larvae are the stick worms so well known to many youthful anglers. The most common species found in lakes all make cases in which they spend their larval life. Most cases are portable, although some are rather small, thin and tube-like, fastened to sticks and stones on the bottom of lakes. The non-mobile larval case is usually small, thus the trout will often ignore it. As a trout food the larva whose home is the portable case is the most important. These larval cases are made from material in the immediate areas, ensuring a ready supply and providing a natural camouflage.

The worm-like larva has hooks on its posterior by which it holds firmly to the case. The body inside the case undulates rhythmically as water circulates over the filament-like gills along the abdomen. If the larva outgrows the case or if the environment undergoes a drastic change, it will leave the case and build another or add new material to the front of the old as the situation warrants. This process may take only a few days.

The larva is omnivorous, largely feeding on plants but sometimes on other insects. The larval state often lasts over two years. As time for pupa-

A thunderstorm such as this one on Stuart Lake will often stimulate fish to strike. Anglers should remember to leave the lake if lightning is present.

tion approaches the insect will seal the end of its case with an open grid-like structure of bits of sticks or weed, often not bothering to remove it from the parent plant. This grid allows sufficient flow of water to supply the necessary oxygen. When the miracle of pupation is accomplished the seal is broken and a new insect of completely different appearance emerges.

The fly patterns known as woolly worms best imitate these larvae and are available in a multitude of color combinations. All are successful in particular situations of environment, in sizes from one-half inch to one and a half inches. Fished with a sinking line, an imitation of this larval stage is a most productive fly.

The technique is not difficult if one is not afraid of hooking weeds occasionally. The fly must rest on the bottom, moving very slowly. If it hangs up, strike it lightly. If it is not a fish make a few fast pulls to clear it of possible weeds, then again let the fly settle, moving it by very slow pulls or letting it rest on the bottom. Wave action will often impart enough movement to the line to give the fly a natural action.

A few species of the sedgefly are free swimmers, carrying their case with them. They swim in a vertical position, rising and falling in the water while moving in erratic circles. The larval cases of these free swimming species are thin, three-thirty-seconds of an inch in diameter and three-quarters of an inch in length, tapering the full length. It is usually made of bits of weed laid parallel to the axis and built spirally. Color is often green with patches of brown.

The free swimming species are best imitated by using a Carey fly pattern with a thin body, taking all but a very few hackle fibres off and shortening the remaining few to about three-eighths inch. The fly should be fished on a floating line, retrieving at a speed sufficient to raise it a short distance and then allowing it again to slowly sink.

Sedgefly—Pupae
Order—TRICHOPTERA

The pupal form of this insect is greatly favored by trout but is little known to the average fly fisherman. The numerous sizes and colors of this aquatic insect and the short period spent in the pupal stage contribute to the lack of information.

When pupation in the case is completed and the new form emerges, it rests for a short time on the bottom before migration to the surface begins. It is never completely at rest, however. The gill filaments on either side of the rear abdomen must continually have water flowing over them to keep the insect supplied with oxygen. For this reason there is a continuous rhythmic undulation of its body.

The head is small with rather large prominent eyes, and attached to either side are long antenna cases which sweep back as long as the body. A short neck joins the head to the large thorax which has six legs on the underside. Two of these legs are designed for swimming and are used much like oars on a boat, the others held tightly to the body. On the upper side of the thorax the cases enclosing the embryo wings angle down either side, sloping to the rear. Its abdomen is narrow at the thorax, becoming wider as it nears the posterior tip, the last three segments becoming large. The gills appear to follow the outer contour of these last segments almost to the extreme tip.

The insect swims to the surface in a long ascending angle and may, before reaching the surface, swim under it for some distance. On reaching the surface a moth-like creature emerges, standing on the now empty pupal case with wings held erect. When the wings dry the insect becomes fully terrestrial.

The colors in pupal form vary widely. There are shades of green, some segmented with yellow bands; others are brown in medium shades, the thorax frequently brown, grey or tan with the body in shades of green.

The Knouff Lake Special is the only commercial fly pattern with which I am familiar that imitates this stage. Many of the Carey patterns can, by thinning the hackle until it is quite sparse, be used successfully.

A sinking tip line will represent the rising pupa effectively by using a rather long retrieve of moderate speed and continuous progress. A floating line used to represent those pupae swimming just under the surface may be retrieved in the same way.

Sedgefly—Terrestrial
Order—TRICHOPTERA

The terrestrial stage of the many species of sedgefly is a valuable part of a trout's diet. It can be seen in early afternoon through late evening on many lakes and ponds through the country. I have seen them emerging before a lake was completely free of ice in spring and, in the lower elevation lakes, well into October.

The emerging sedge is a moth-like insect with wings held erect while drying. The wings are soon lowered where they are held tent-like over the body, being broad at the outer ends and tapering to the thorax. When at rest the inner edges are held together over the body, sloping sharply to leave no visible abdomen and are considerably longer than the body. In the air sedgeflies appear to have a heavy body and are clumsy fliers.

They often run erratically on the water, leaving a tiny wake, or jump and pirouette, fly a short distance and again do their dance. Often they will leave the water for the shore-line trees where birds feed on them in the air.

In size these insects are from one-quarter inch to one and one half inches. The wings are cinnamon, beige, brown, grey and mottled combinations of these colors. The bodies are shades of brown and also green.

The list of fly patterns to imitate this insect is endless, many are referred to as "sedge." A few examples are Green Sedge, Brown Sedge and Beaver Sedge, among others. One of the most successful representations, though, is not identified as a sedge pattern and is not especially representative of it. It is the Tom Thumb, in various sizes a most productive pattern when the sedgefly is active.

Although all types of lines are used in fishing these imitations, a possible exception is the Tom Thumb which is used most frequently on a floating line. Since this fly is constructed of deer hair which is hollow, it floats extremely well. It is, however, somewhat fragile and soon damaged, making it useless. For this reason keep a supply on hand so as not to be embarrassed if the fish are rising well.

A wet line should be used in a manner that will impart movement to imitate a spent insect which sinks to the bottom but occasionally tries to reach the surface again. To simulate this action, retrieve 10 to 15 inches of line with slight pauses, then let sink for 10 to 20 seconds and repeat. Fish the line slowly right to the leader.

A floating line is used mainly with the Tom Thumb or fly patterns designed to float. Let it sit on the water for a short time, every 20 seconds or so twitching enough to create a slight disturbance around the fly. Retrieve with a fast continuous recovery for a short distance and again let it rest for a few seconds.

Back Swimmer

Order—NOTONECTA

This insect is so similar in general appearance and habit to the water boatman (*Corixa*) that it would be needless to repeat, other than to note those differences important to the fly fisherman.

It is much larger than the water boatman, being one-half to five-eighths inches long, broad at the head and about half way along the body curving and tapering to the abdominal tip.

Since the back swimmer swims upside down — hence its name — it carries its air bubble on its back, giving it a silvery appearance in the water on the underside. The belly is black with light tan, and brown V-shaped markings on the back. It is a thick bodied insect whose nuptial activity is similar to the water boatman.

It is of little importance until late August and September, often into October, when the nuptial flight occurs. At this time it leaves the water to fly rather clumsily at good speed, only to land again and swim to the bottom.

Flies such as the Doc Spratley and any small silver bodied Carey work well, as does any fly with much silver in the dressing. Fish rather fast on a sinking line, #2 density, or dead drift on a floating line with enough of the leader treated with flotation dressing to hold the fly two or three inches under water.

Flies

Commercial Patterns and Changes

On the following three pages are a selection of commercially available flies which have been trimmed to represent some of the insects described in this chapter on feeding habits:

Original Flies   # Altered Patterns

Olive green #10 Wooly Worm: By trimming off the top hackle, the
wooly worm becomes a reasonable shrimp pattern.

Yellow Sally #10 or #12 wet fly. With the wing cut off and the
hackle spread to the sides it makes a reasonable damselfly nymph.

Maroon Carey #8 with the hackle thinned out to represent a blood leech.

Yellow Hackle #12 wet fly with the hackle trimmed off top and bottom
represents a water boatman.

62

Original Flies   # Altered Patterns

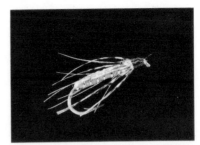

*Red Carey #10 with hackle thinned to 10 or 12 strands, just enough
to impart a life-like movement of the natural blood worm.*

*Doc Spratley #8 with wing cut back to better represent a nymphal wing
case. (Dragonfly nymph.)*

*Col' Carey #8. Thin the hackle but not the tail to give a more
leech-like appearance to represent a brown leech.*

*Knouff Lake Special. Trim top off the hackle and it will better imitate
the pupal stage of the traveller sedgefly. (Sedge pupae.)*

Original Flies   # Altered Patterns

*Tom Thumb #10. Work cement into the tips of the hackle wing and when
tacky pull together with the tail. Then trim to look like a sedge on the water's surface.*

*March Brown Wet Fly #12. Cut off the wing, leaving a short stub to represent the wing
case. Reduce the tail to a few fibres and curve slightly to represent a mayfly nymph.*

   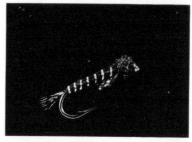

*Doc Spratley #12. As a chironamidae pupae, remove the wing entirely
and cut the hackle very short.*

*This Fullback #10 represents many
species of beetle larvae.*   *The Halfback is a general nymph pattern.
Useful in all sizes.*

## CHAPTER NINE

The Rise

Rising fish tell a story if one watches them and discovers the pattern. The rise, for instance, indicates if the fish are feeding on nymphs, pupae or dry flies. Even the absence of fish rising offers clues to their probable activity.

In early spring fish often move in long low arcs, sometimes close to the surface and moving fast, leaving a slight wake. Seldom do they completely leave the water. This short, low, lazy arc is often seen in late morning through the afternoon, particularly in late May, June and into July.

This activity is the result of a nymphing rise, often mistaken for a dry fly rise. Many pupal forms are taken in this manner in the early part of the season, damsel and mayfly nymphs in the later part. The fish taking these insect forms close to the surface come up over the top and take them on the way down. This rise is easily confused with the dry rise, the main difference being the speed of execution. The fish's nymphing rise is rather lazy; its dry rise much quicker and often higher.

The high clearing arc is the true dry fly rise. During this rise fish moving to the surface will at times take the fly while coming up; at other times they come over the top, taking it going down. It is not unusual for fish to land on a fly, turn back and pick up the now sunken insect. Such action is often seen with the larger sedge flies in July and August. It is also present on the rare occasions when fish are feeding on terrestrial damselflies. The fish will rise against a weed lined with damselflies, knocking them to the water then coming back to pick them up.

The novice dry-fly fisherman misses many fish owing to this time lapse between the rise and the actual taking of the fly. The solution is don't strike. Instead, lift the line to remove the slack so the fish takes the fly on a tight line, creating its own strike. Sometimes it is beneficial to count off two or three seconds before lifting the rod tip to remove slack line.

Another condition is a swirl just under the surface with no fish seen. While this is not a true rise it does indicate near surface activity and is most often seen in still evenings in July or August. The large sedge pupae swim-

To a novice a rising fish such as this one at Lodgepole Lake arouses eager anticipation. A veteran, however, knows that rising fish are not necessarily biting fish.

ming close to the surface are followed by the fish well underneath. There is the rise and swift turn, taking the pupae head first on the way down again. The back swimmer is also taken in this manner during the intense activity of these insects in September and October.

Dimpling is seen when fish come to the surface picking up small dipterous pupae, usually during still evenings. The occasional fish's head is seen momentarily, only to drop under the surface again, leaving a little ring like a heavy raindrop. Pupae of many insects and spent terrestrials are taken in this way.

Another type of trout activity — and one that arouses eager anticipation on the part of novice anglers — is the result of fish in many lakes being the host for parasitic copepods. Fish infected with these parasites are referred to as lousy. While the infestation doesn't affect edibility, it must cause some discomfort since fish so infected leap high in the air and land heavily on their sides in an effort to dislodge them. Unfortunately for eager novices, this activity is not indicative of feeding activity and is ignored by experienced anglers.

A lack of rising fish can be just as significant as if the lake were dimpled with rises. Frequently during a good hatch there are very few, if any, fish rising. It is possible the fish are taking nymphs near the bottom, particularly on bright sunny days. Another trout characteristic to remember is that during an extended hatch of one particular insect, they will on occasion seem to tire of them and feed on shrimp for a few days.

For the aforementioned reasons close observation of the various types of rises and the general activity of trout at all times will improve your sport immensely.

66

## CHAPTER TEN

The Strike

The strike is when a fish takes the imitation offered by the angler. It is the highlight of fly fishing, making the heart pound and the adrenalin flow. It matters not whether the fisherman is experienced or a novice, the electrifying strike of a good fish is always a new experience. While to the novice it may be just another strike, the pro knows differently. The way a fish takes a fly tells much of what is happening below the surface. A hard solid strike, a gentle pick or just the slightest occasional line movement — each relates its own story.

Often in lakes with a good fish population the strike is hard and positive, followed by a ferocious run and leap. Fish that strike in this manner are most often in the three-quarter pound to one-and-a-half pound class. They have not yet become independent to the point where they travel or feed in small groups but school in fair numbers. Thus the competition for food is great. Any individual that decides your fly is a desirable morsel does not hesitate for fear of being beaten to it, hence the hard, positive strike.

Another type of strike which is often experienced rarely produces a fish. It is most exasperating because the fly fisherman is inclined to keep working the same fly in the same way. This strike is the double rap, never hard but very fast. I have often heard fishermen say, "How can they take a fly that hard and not get hooked?"

The truth is that they don't take the fly. The strike, if indeed we can call it such, is caused by the fish coming to it quite fast, then at the last second deciding it is not what it was thought to be and turning quickly away. Water turbulence as the fish turns rapidly is what gives the rapid double strike. At these times a fish is occasionally hooked in the cheek or some other part of the body, but rarely in the mouth.

When this situation arises it is advisable to change flies but stay in the same pattern. Both smaller and larger patterns should be tried, or color changed. Experimenting will often produce the right fly.

Another strike frequently encountered is referred to as pecking, or beaking. It is identified by a single light fast rap and seems only to happen two or three times over a short period. Then there is either no more action or the strike becomes solid. On rare occasions this type of strike will continue over a long period and the fish will be hooked but easily lost. Landed fish will often have the hook in the tip of the upper or lower lip and be lightly hooked.

This is the fish's "no interest" strike, done a short time before starting to feed or when the feeding period has ended. If the latter and it is late in the day you may as well go home. It's all over.

At other times there is one of the most exciting of all strikes, the one that is responsible for continued freedom for many very large fish. This strike is identified by the fly suddenly stopping, much as if one has hooked a sunken log. When the line is tightened to see if it will pull loose there is no movement, and the leader is in danger of parting. Suddenly, there is rapid movement of the line as a fish shakes its head in annoyance and proceeds to add another fly to an undoubtedly large collection.

In this situation it is much better policy to just set the hook then let nearly all tension off the line for 10 to 15 seconds to see if it will move. Fish hooked in this manner usually start to move relatively slowly, then increase speed as the friction of water on the line builds up. At this point an apprehensive eye is kept on the reel as backing quickly diminishes till the fish breaks the surface in a high twisting leap. Thereafter line is recovered and lost as short runs become shorter until the prize comes to net.

There is a type of strike that is not really a strike but rather an intuitive feeling that there is a fish at the fly. A fish, slowly cruising, picks up the imitation, usually of a pupal form of gnat or midge that is very slow moving, discovers the error and immediately spits it out. Rarely does this type of strike register as far as the rod handle, except if in spitting out the fly the fish inadvertently gets hooked in the skin of its lip. Such a fish is often lost owing to such light hooking.

Line movement where it enters the water is the key to solid hooking of these fish. Immediately the slightest unusual movement of line is detected the hook must be set. Fish hooked in this manner are often close to the boat and come straight up a few times then run. This situation has on many occasions resulted in fish jumping into the boat and at other times completely over it, often to run under the boat or foul the anchor rope.

When large flies are being used another type of strike is the already mentioned gentle tug, tug. Fish, mistaking these flies for leeches, come from behind and suck them in, but the fly being fixed to a line will not move backwards. The tendency on the part of the fisherman is to retrieve all line and make another cast. When this happens a few times it is thought the dressing is too long and the fish is missing the hook. The fly dressing is accordingly shortened and the fly ruined. The solution is to ignore the tug, tug except for a gentle set of the hook. Then continue the retrieve normally. Fish will often swim a short way and come back, taking the fly from the side or even head on. On the second strike there is no doubt as it is taken solidly, the fish often being hooked well back in the mouth.

## CHAPTER ELEVEN

Tricks and Strategy

Anchoring a boat to best advantage is a very important detail usually not given much thought. An anchor of about 10 pounds is sufficient to hold most car-top boats if a rope of about 50 feet is used. This length will give an angle on the rope in 30 feet of water that will be secure in any wind in which it is possible to fly fish comfortably.

Whenever possible keep in such a position as not to be directly over an area where fish travel back and forth to feed but rather where this path can be covered with the fly line. Throwing an anchor overboard will spook fish for some time and will often put large fish away for the day. Decide where you are going to anchor then lower the anchor to within a few feet of the bottom. Drift or row into the desired position and lower it the remaining distance. Let out the amount of slack that will be required to get an angle sufficient to hold and you are ready to fish. If you move, do it with as little disturbance as possible. Your fellow anglers will appreciate it and your own sport will be improved.

Remember that most car-top boats have rivets that can be very sharp or ribs that are raised off the bottom where a line, if stepped on, can be severely damaged. Dirt and oil also accumulate in the bottom of many boats and are not only injurious to the lines but affect the sinking or floating quality of them. Any piece of heavy material, used as a mat, offers ample protection and is easily shaken clean of sand or gravel and washed. It also effectively covers crevices and obstructions in which a line can foul when paying out off the bottom of the boat.

By wearing soft-soled shoes the angler is less likely to injure his line or slip in the boat if he stands to cast. I have a pair of low gumboots cut down to about 10 inches high, an ideal boat boot. They are easily removed and help keep feet dry when launching. In an emergency they will also serve as bailing cans.

Remember, also, that in rainy weather, even with waterproof pants and jacket, a pool of water will form in a cushion. Sitting in this water is most uncomfortable, even though your body is dry. Fortunately, a comfortable, soft seat in which water cannot form a puddle can easily be made with some nylon rope and a few pieces of one by three or two by four lumber.

Make a square frame of the lumber, on edge, about 12 by 16 inches, 3 or 4 inches deep. Drill holes in the sides and ends about one inch apart and one-half inch down from the upper edge. Then thread a rope through the holes length-wise, then from the sides, crossing the first ropes in a basket weave. The resulting grid is quite comfortable and water runs through, eliminating any chance of a puddle.

Rarely do you see an old pro standing in a boat while fishing. There are a number of good reasons. When fishing close to others, by sitting and keeping your hands low between your legs you can hide the retrieve, thus not divulging any secrets. It is also much easier to watch the rod tip and it can be held much steadier. As a consequence, the little movements a nymphing fish makes that do not signal to the rod handle can be struck in time to hook them. Sitting is also safer and a lot easier on the legs.

When a good fish is hooked and line is paying out fast, however, it is often an advantage to stand until it is under control. Line that has been stripped into the boat and lying coiled on the bottom will sometimes tangle as it comes up to the rod. Standing gives more distance from the rod to the coiled line. If a tangle should come off the bottom there is considerably more time to shake it out before it hits the first guide.

Another advantage of keeping the rod high with the tip well up is that more line is kept out of the water. The result is less friction between line and water, so often responsible for breaking light leaders on large, fast moving fish. Once the fish is under control, sit down. It is less likely to run very far again if you or your shadow are not seen, particularly when fishing shallow water.

Here a point to remember concerns the hard-hitting fish that seem to take when the line is short, just coming up off the bottom and breaking you off. This snapped line can often be prevented by holding the line differently. Instead of retrieving line between the thumb and first finger hold it between the second and third fingers. Unless your hand is closed into a fist, it is impossible to put so much pressure on the line, even if surprised, that it will freeze the line and break a fish off.

Netting and Releasing

The antics inexperienced anglers perform when netting a good fish I find very amusing. The larger the fish, the greater the excitement — and the less chance of success. When the fish nears the boat a frantic swoop with the net usually misses. The fish, now understandably in a panic, does all it can to stay as far as possible from the boat and the net. Not infrequently the wild sweep of the net breaks the fish off, or an excited attempt to hold it close to the boat puts too much strain on the leader with the same result. The tyro then slumps in the boat, speechless and dejected, looking around for someone to blame.

Knowing how to net a fish properly is an important aspect of a successful trip. Most fish are lost at the boat. One way to prevent this unhappy situation is to bring the fish to the net, above. Do not "chase" the fish with the net.

A fish should be played carefully until it is tired and lies on its side. The net is then wetted so that it will bag properly, held in the water and the fish gently led head first into it. Only then is the net lifted.

For a number of reasons it is desirable at times to release fish. Small fish and spawners, for instance, should always be set free if the sport of fly fishing is to remain of maximum enjoyment to all. Many fly fishermen keep only exceptionally fine specimens, or enough for a meal or two, releasing all others. Fish caught on a fly and released carefully have a very high survival rate as opposed to other methods of fishing. Those that have been caught but have escaped the table one way or another in their youth are doubtless among the large fish taken annually.

Small trout can be released easily by running the hand down the leader to the fly and tipping it up, shaking the fish off. If deeply hooked, it is best to net it, wet the hands, and while in the net hold firmly with as little pressure as possible. Still in the net, put the fish in the water and turn the net over. The small fellow will be little the worse for the experience and very much smarter.

Large fish should always be netted, and with wet hands freed of the hook. Keep fingers and hands out of the gills to avoid injuring the fish and killing it. As before, put the net and fish in the water and turn the net over to release.

A Kamloops trout in spawning condition is a very poor quality table fish. The flesh is pale, soft and unappetizing. Spawners are easily recognized by their dark color, red gill plates and red down each side. The female does not display this deep coloration as often as the male. Males, however, because of their more aggressive nature are taken on the fly more frequently than the females. Spawners of both sexes do not fight well. They are sluggish, not the aerial acrobats normal for fish in good condition.

All spawners should be released unharmed, using the same technique as for larger fish — with the following exception. Since spawners are low in vitality, after a long fight it is advisable to make sure the gills are working or the fish will die. Before turning the net over, take the fish by the tail and move it gently back and forth in the water until it makes an effort to swim away. Still holding the fish by the tail take the net clear of the head then release.

Rain Gear

Rain gear is a must for everyone who frequents the lakes. Nothing will spoil a holiday or fishing trip like rain if one is not able to keep dry. Modern rain clothing is light, a full suit of pants and hooded jacket taking up less space than a one-pound chocolate box. A few large plastic garbage bags also take little room and are invaluable for keeping fly boxes, lunches, cameras and other items dry.

Insects

A good way to become familiar with insects that fish feed on is to examine their stomach contents. It not only tells you the insects they are eating, but also the color and size in relation to the time of year. This information can be kept as a reference for the following years.

Opening fish for stomach examinations I find slow, messy and often inconvenient. My solution is a small, saucer-like white container that holds about an inch of water, and a small spoon-like instrument about 8 to 10 inches long. This instrument can be made from a piece of aluminum or copper wire three-sixteenths diameter, one end flattened, made hollow and smoothed off. The spoon end should be about a fifteen degree angle from the handle, one-inch long and a half-inch wide, slightly hollowed. It is put down the fish's throat in a turning motion into the stomach. After withdrawing, the contents are put into the dish of water and stirred to separate the material for examination.

If desired a few of the good specimens may be put in vials for better observation and study. Because insects removed from a fish deteriorate rapidly, do your observations quickly for obvious reasons.

When looking for insect life in the water, the surface attracts so much of your attention that your eyes focus there. Since small nymphs and pupae are difficult to see at any time, even for those well trained in their observation, the average person sees nothing below the surface. The trick is to focus from one to two feet beneath the surface. Then when an insect is seen it can be followed to the surface and emergence watched closely. With small flies that hatch in this manner the time from arrival at the surface as a pupa to when they fly as a terrestrial is only a matter of seconds. If the pupa is not seen before it reaches the surface about all that is noticed is a fly sitting on the water, the actual emerging missed entirely.

Active and Inactive Periods

All wildlife, including insects, have periods of rest and periods of activity which vary under differing circumstances. Moon cycles and weather patterns largely affect the degree of activity. Such domestic animals as horses and cattle are often very restless when certain weather changes approach. Animals with more nocturnal habits, including fish, are greatly affected by moon phases. The activity of birds, horses and cattle will often give clues as to what one may expect on the lakes.

When ducks, blackbirds and other wildfowl are resting you may be sure the fish are too. If many cattle or horses are lying down or standing in the shade of trees, you may as well do the same, or at least don't expect too much from your fishing efforts. On the other hand, if all is activity and you are not raising any fish, take a long look at your techniques and your equipment. Something in wrong.

In late June and through July there are frequent thunderstorms with short periods of heavy rain and sometimes wind. These heavy showers last from fifteen minutes to three-quarters of an hour, then the sun comes out and all is bright, warm and quiet. This sequence may occur three or four times in an afternoon. This type of day can be the most productive if one is not afraid of rain and heads for shore if the thunderstorm includes lightning. Remember that lightning strikes the highest object and an angler in the boat is the highest object on a lake!

Many times, a few minutes after the rain starts, I will have the lake all to myself. Where there is a good size tree boats will be pulled ashore, the owners standing huddled under the branches trying to avoid getting wet. Shortly after the rain begins the fish become very active and continue until the rain stops. Thereafter all is quiet except for the boats leaving the protection of the trees.

I look around for signs of another shower with anticipation. Although the last deluge produced three or four beautiful fish, there will be little more action until the next rain comes. How do I know? An approaching raincloud of this type depresses the barometer until the storm is directly overhead. Then barometric pressure starts a rapid rise and fish become very active. As the storm passes, the pressure steadies and activity ceases until the next rapid rise.

The observant angler will at times notice a localized activity of fish. On tree-lined lakes it is usually off a point of land or a wooded island. At these times there is often a fair wind and the activity will be to the lee of the point or island. The reason is that flying ants are being blown into the water. They are usually large black ants that do not really float on the surface but rather in it, being partly submerged. A stout bodied, wet imitation with a grey or pale tan hackle treated to float and fished on a dry line dead drift, will often produce well.

On meadow or rangeland lakes activity is usually caused by an off-shore wind which blows bees or grasshoppers out over the water. If the wind is gusty the activity of fish increases or decreases with wind velocity, proving that the fish are feeding on these aforementioned insects. I might add that when fish have had a good feed of ants they are seldom active for two or three days. The very tough exoskeleton of these insects requires some time to digest.

"Wind from the east, fish bite the least," is an old adage among fishermen. I have found it to be quite true, seldom having had a good day when the wind blew from the east. However, there are times when the wind is fairly strong and "slicks" are seen on the water surface. These slicks, or quiet water, may be where a point of land or an island breaks the wind, the slick being on the down-wind side of these obstructions. At other times they may form in the main body of the lake — long narrow areas of flat quiet water.

Anchoring in a position to cast across these slicks but keeping the boat out of them often produces a good fish. After having taken one or two fish from a slick, look for another, keeping in mind the normal feeding areas and confine your operations to them. Three or four such slicks may be productive all day by working them in rotation. Take care not to over-work any one, as the fish may spook and not return. Slicks are no guarantee of fish, but do offer the best chance under poor conditions.

Trollers

Few things annoy a fly fisherman more than a thoughtless troller. Fortunate-

A "slick" at the west end of
Francois Lake in Central B.C.

ly, most are considerate and avoid interference and resultant ill feelings. Annoying experiences probably are due to lack of understanding the simple requirements of a fly fisherman at anchor.

The area of water a fly fisherman at anchor uses is restricted by length of his fly line, the maximum of which is 35 yards. There are very few indeed who use this much line, 20 to 25 yards being more realistic. For this reason a circle of 50 to 60 yards is all the water that can be covered from a boat at anchor. Some trollers continually invade this water with no thought for the disastrous effect it has on the fly fisherman's sport. They may be offended when it is brought to their attention — at times rather vigorously.

A boat moving through this area, particularly with an outboard motor, will often put the fish away for a very lengthy period. When it happens close to the end of a feeding period they frequently do not return. This thoughtless action on the part of trollers may sometimes be used to advantage, although I do not feel that it completely offsets the disadvantage. A boat trolling into the area often is moving fish ahead of it.

To take advantage of this situation, cast into the path of the troller and allow the line to sink well before starting to retrieve. Frequently the result is a good fish. It requires some caution as the line must not at any time be under the approaching boat since there would be danger of damaging the line. The moving fish seem to be about 30 to 40 feet in front and moving to the side of the intruding craft. With a little practice the percentage of success is amazing.

Water Current

Water current is important to the angler because insect life of slow movement tends to drift with it. Fish taken when the fly is presented in a particular direction only are often a result of this current. Water movement at a depth, however, is very difficult to detect and its direction may be opposite to that on the surface. One clue is a sinking line that shows a tendency to drift in a direction other than that from which the wind is blowing. When this natural deep drift is noted anchor the boat in such a position to take advantage of it. Ignore surface conditions because the bottom is where the fish feed and they normally have little concern with the surface.

Fish Repellents

Once, after three good days on a lake with a friend who hadn't done too well, he offered me an orange. I refused.

"What's the matter, don't you like oranges?" he asked.

"Sure," I replied, "but not when I'm fishing."

"Okay, how come?"

"Well," I said, "I can smell an orange a hundred yards away, and if I get that on my hands it gets on my flies, and I don't think the fish like it."

"After three days you tell me that!" he exclaimed, stowing the orange back in his lunch box.

From then on he did much better, but I don't think he ever forgave me for not telling him sooner. Any strong smell such as citrous fruits, oil, onion sandwich — a favorite of mine — tobacco and insect repellent or lotion are definitely offensive to fish.

Muddy Fish

Over the years I have listened to a great number of recipes for taking the sometimes muddy taste out of trout. These recipes involve everything from skinning them, taking the fat off, soaking in vinegar and smoking. None, I find, will work. Muddy fish are the result of feed at certain times of the year and the flavor pervades the fish.

It occurs in late summer after the fish have been feeding on snails and leeches for some time. Snails live on the algae on rocks and plants on the lake bottom. Leeches feed largely on snails, and the fluids of dead organisms in the water. In addition, some species of sedge make their larval cases out of a species of weed that has a pungent and offensive odor.

A prolonged diet of any of these organisms will seriously affect the otherwise fine flavor of trout. If this muddiness is not too bad, it may be hidden by smoking but it certainly cannot be removed. Fish that are strongly muddy can usually be detected as soon as they are in the net. They should be released to be caught again, larger and probably of good quality.

Caring for Fish

Many fish, particularly during hot summer weather, are so poorly cared for they become inedible. Some fish that are referred to as being "muddy' or with "belly burn" are, in fact, in early stages of decay. This condition is evident when the fish is cleaned — the ribs separate from the flesh which is soft and somewhat mushy.

Keeping fish in a firm wholesome condition is simple, inexpensive and takes up little room in even a small boat. A cooler is the secret.

Most fish camps have ice with many offering a deep freeze service. As a substitute for ice on a day trip, freezer packs that can be kept in a deep freeze are excellent. They can be frozen again and again, will last for many years and can be kept clean by simply washing after use. In a good cooler they will hold an adequately low temperature, under ordinary conditions, for two days or more if the ratio of fish to ice is reasonable.

There are many coolers on the market — plastic, metal and styrofoam — in a variety of shapes and sizes. Styrofoam coolers are the least expensive but also the least durable. They are, however, so inexpensive that when they become too soiled to clean easily or damaged so that efficiency is impaired, replacement won't likely break the bank.

A jute fibre potato sack washed and bleached completes the equipment necessary to keep fish in excellent table condition.

In use, two or three frozen ice packs are placed in the bottom of the cooler. The potato sack is soaked in cold water, wrung out and laid on top of the ice packs to prevent the fish getting freezer burn. Place the fish on the sack then fold the sack over the fish to keep them moist.

After the fish have been removed the sack can be easily washed and hung to dry. About every third use, bleach added to the water will keep the sack clean and sweet smelling. Sprinkle a little baking soda in the cooler after it is rinsed out, put it away with the lid ajar so air can circulate, and you will always have fish of the best possible quality.

If you don't have a cooler on your boat and if the weather is cool, a temporary substitue is a wet cloth of open weave or burlap placed over the fish. Through evaporation it will keep them relatively cool, although the material must be kept wet.

The worst possible way ever conceived to keep fish is a "stringer."

Below are rainbow from Dutch Lake on Highway 5 north of Kamloops. Unfortunately, they are on a stringer, according to the author " the worst possible way to keep fish."

While on the lake he uses a cooler, opposite, and freezer packs.

This device consists of a chain with snaps which look like large safety pins. The stringer is tied to the side of the boat, fish are hooked to the chain by the lower jaw and dragged along in the water. Often they are not even killed but left to die a slow, cruel death.

In addition, the warm surface water and oil scum from outboard motors and algae doesn't exactly enhance the flavor of a fish already decaying on the stringer. For excellent quality fish throw the stringer in the garbage pail and substitute a cooler and ice.

Smoking Fish

Split the fish from the inside along the full length of the backbone and lay flat.

Mix one part pickling salt to two parts Demerara sugar. Cover the flesh side generously with this mixture and place skin side down in a glass, plastic, or enamel container. Do not use aluminum or steel. The container should be just big enough to hold the fish in a somewhat confined position. They will then make their own brine.

Don't be in a hurry to add water. Let the fish make their own brine as much as they will, then add enough water to cover. Put a weight on to hold them under and rearrange them two or three times while in the brine. Twelve to fourteen hours should be long enough in the brine. Then wash them well, pat dry and put in the smokehouse skin side down. If metal racks are used, rub the fish lightly with a cloth saturated in oil or fat. This keeps them from sticking to the racks and tearing the flesh when removed.

Do not use birch or pear wood when smoking since the fish will taste sour if birch is used and bitter with pear. Also do not use wood with bark on. It puts a black deposit on the fish. Use dry wood instead of green which, like bark, will often leave a black residue on the fish. Cottonwood, alder, cherry and hickory all produce a nicely-flavored fish.

The smokehouse I use is made of plywood with a sheet metal bottom. For heat I use an element from an electric stove adapted as a hot plate, the control switch on the outside. The cabinet is 4 feet high by 2 feet square. A smoke spreader is 1 foot square, sheet metal, and suspended approximately 1 foot above the fuel pan by a chain. Finally, at the upper end of the cabinet are three trays made of small size poultry netting spaced 5 inches apart. A 10-inch cake pan holds the wood chips on the element.

The length of smoking time varies with the size, degree of heat and how moist a product is desired. To smoke fish that weigh up to 2 pounds I set the heat switch to about medium for some 6 hours. Time in the smokehouse controls the flavor and heat controls the moisture content. If you find the smoke flavor too strong, decrease the time in the smokehouse and increase the heat. If the fish are too moist increase the heat and/or extend the time. A bit of experimenting and juggling will produce a fish with the flavor and moisture suited to your own taste.

## CHAPTER TWELVE

The Fishing Season

The first insects to appear in the spring that are of significance to the fisherman are the water boatmen, followed a few weeks later by the first important midges. There are smaller species which appear earlier but are of little interest to the size of the fish the fly fisherman seeks to catch. Just before the first of June gnats appear and for some weeks are often seen in large numbers. At this point damselflies, mayflies and some small species of sedgeflies are hatching. Later still, dragonflies appear in good numbers and the larger sedgeflies that attract so much attention from the fish and fisherman in later summer evenings. Then, usually in late August or early September when days are bright and sunny and there is light frost at night, the back swimmers appear and occupy the fish well into October.

It is then fish will start a concentrated search for shrimp and the occasional leech. This search will continue until freeze-up with the possible late hatch of gnats attracting them for a time and, during the occasional year, a very late mayfly hatch.

The hatches frequently overlap in mid-season. At this time the fisherman who can recognize the various hatches has an advantage over less knowledgeable colleagues. His knowledge saves much time and eliminates much guessing.

For instance, most fly fishermen have a great many flies of all sizes and color combinations. Since it is not possible to properly try all these patterns in a short time, a good knowledge of insects may immediately eliminate all but a half dozen and necessitate only a few changes before finding the right fly. Late-season hatches are usually sparse, and sighting only one insect in the terrestrial form often provides the key to a successful day.

When no insect life is visible on the surface it is wise to use shrimp, leech and dragonfly nymph patterns. These are the insects on which fish feed when emergent pupae and nymphs are not available. Shrimp are the bread and potatoes of fish. But, as humans get tired of this diet, so do fish get tired of shrimp. In late season they have already been on a sporadic diet of shrimp and the few emergent nymphs and pupae of late hatches are taken greedily for variety.

Every year there is a period when trout go off feed. Some years it will last up to six weeks, more often three or four weeks, usually between mid-July and mid-August. This condition does not mean fish cannot be taken but a fly fisherman must use all his knowledge to catch a few. During this period the stomachs of fish are small, hard, shrunken and usually quite empty. There may be a few shrimp, perhaps the odd snail and possibly a few gnat or midge, all of which will constitute little in volume and nothing to indicate a feeding pattern.

Deep water off a shoal where the sharp break-off forms a shadow near the bottom, or where shoreline trees cast a shadow on the water in late afternoon, are likely places to fish. From sundown to dark, near shoal areas are frequently productive.

About mid-August or earlier, depending on lake elevation, fish become active in late afternoon when the large sedge flies start to emerge. From then on activity increases following their general pattern and fishing improves with only minor lapses until freeze up.

Garibaldi Lake in Garibaldi Provincial Park. Like many B.C. lakes, it was barren until 1932 when rainbow were introduced. They now spawn naturally and provide excellent sport, especially on a dry fly. By the way, Garibaldi Lake is a one-hour hike, all uphill.

## CHAPTER THIRTEEN

Spawning

Spawning is the natural process of reproduction in trout, the successful fulfilment of which is fraught with many problems and hazards of which man is not the least. As already noted, a spawning trout is easily recognized and to some extent protected by law, as it should be. Coloration is distinctive and not easily confused with naturally dark colored fish. The overall dark skintone, the bright pink to red gill plates and lateral line are all indicative of this condition. It is rare indeed that a fish in this condition will provide the energetic leaping and fighting for which the Kamloops trout is noted. Usually slow and sluggish, rarely more than just breaking the water surface, it soon gives up and comes to net.

Very early in the spring, often before the ice is completely off the lake, these fish cruise the shoreline, frequently in very shallow water as they look for a flowing stream of desirable ecological character. Here they will travel upstream for long distances to a suitable location where the eggs are deposited and fertilized. The fish then return to the lake where they soon regain condition and are once more worthy opponents for any sportsman.

The foregoing is the usual sequence in an ideal situation. However, conditions frequently are less than ideal, owing to the nature of the lakes in which the fish were stocked.

Not all lakes have suitable streams in which the fish can spawn, others have no streams, yet are capable of sustaining good fish populations. Some have adequate streams with all the required necessities except a flow of sufficient water of long enough duration to permit the return of fry to the lake. In wet years some of these lakes will have good natural returns, at other times little, if any, reproduction. This type of lake is most difficult for those agencies responsible for maintaining fish populations at a safe density and of a reasonable size. The erratic conditions of these lakes require constant surveillance and census of fish population and condition in order to insure an adequate food supply to maintain a normal growth rate.

Lakes that have no natural spawning facilities are most easily controll-

Fisheries Enhancement Project

The spawning habitat of the Little Horsefly River was increased through a cooperative project between the Ministry of Environment, Fish and Wildlife Branch and the Ministry of Highways.
Kokanee and Rainbow Trout now utilize this once unproductive area ensuring fish for the future.

Province of British Columbia Ministry of Environment

Enhancement of destroyed or unproductive streams such as the Little Horsefly River, above, is inexpensive for benefits gained and ensures future generations excellent fishing. Unfortunately, such conservation projects have a low priority with the B.C. Government. Equally unfortunate is the attitude of many people who molest and even catch spawning fish which are useless as food.

ed. General size and condition at any given time will indicate the stocking requirements from year to year to maintain a balance of fish to available food.

A number of lakes that have streams conducive to spawning runs have fish traps where the eggs are taken from the females and fertilized with milt from the males. They are then transported to hatcheries where the eggs are hatched. After the tiny fish reach a suitable size they are released into lakes throughout the country to grow in a natural wild environment.

In some lakes, being devoid of any stream, the fish are unable to get rid of the spawn and "clean up" as it is called. These fish will maintain a poor condition for a long time, rarely becoming prime fish.

It is a great shame that many unthinking people, ignorant of the way of trout, molest them in the normally shallow streams where they spawn, senselessly poking them with sticks or throwing stones at them and in some cases netting them. They are practically useless as food in spawning condition, having soft flesh and a poor flavor. If left unmolested, they and their progeny could add more to the enjoyment of the outdoors for these same people than will the dubious exercise of interfering with the cycle of trout reproduction.

## CHAPTER FOURTEEN

The Effect of Light

Light is the prime energy source of all life. None of the existing biological forms of plant or animal life could hope to survive without it, and the vitally required heat, food, oxygen and energy would be nonexistent. Every year, new discoveries are made relating to the properties of light and the effect on our daily existence.

As fly fishermen we are only concerned with the mechanics of light that affect trout in the lakes we fish. Everyone is familiar with refraction of light, as it is a quality of light studied in school at an early age, usually demonstrated by placing a pencil at an angle in a glass of water. The pencil appears to be broken at the water line and offset from that above the water. The portion within the water also appears larger in diameter owing to the magnification of this medium.

Water is much more dense than air and light speed is slowed down as it enters the water at an angle, bending toward the vertical plane. The shorter the light rays, the more they approach the vertical, therefore the short rays penetrate water more deeply than do the longer light rays. Red rays are long and do not bend as readily as the shorter yellow, green or blue. For this reason red has no great penetration in water.

The summer sun moving northward compacts the light rays and they are shorter, now penetrating deeply into the water. Since fish like a rather dim twilight condition, they move down to a comfortable light level. In very clear lakes it is not unusual that fish will go to a depth that puts them out of reach of the fly fisherman during daylight hours. The dark water lakes, and those that often look like thin soup, having much algae at or near the surface, fare much better. Light not penetrating to any great depth, the fish will be comparatively close to the surface and more easily within reach.

As the fall season approaches, the sun is now in its southward journey. The rays, no longer compressed, become longer and do not penetrate the water to the previous depth. The fish begin to move up as the light fades

Lakes such as Stake, above, are numerous and productive throughout Interior B.C.

and continue to do so as the angle of light changes with the south-moving sun.

Very large fish that have all summer been in deep water during daylight hours are now moving within reach. In addition, those that spawned in the spring are now in good condition, a prize worthy of the fisherman's skill and ability.

Fish do not like the sun or bright light in their eyes any more than we do, thus fishing into the sun so that your fly tends to come from the side or the rear of the fish is often an advantage.

Winter and Summer Kill

This phenomenon, fortunately, does not occur with any great frequency. Winter kill is prevalent in certain lakes, occurring every few years, while other lakes are rarely, if ever, affected. Insufficient oxygen to sustain life in trout is the basic cause of winter kill; however, causes may vary.

The main sources of oxygen in a lake are derived from aeration by the wind, inflowing streams and the plants on the lake bottom that convert light to oxygen through a process known as photosynthesis. During the hours of daylight, particularly on sunny days, the green plants on the lake bottom give off oxygen in the form of minute bubbles that rise in tiny strings through the water.

The ice of winter reduces the light in varying degrees depending on ice quality and eliminates the effect of wind aeration. Snow on the ice further reduces light and eliminates the photosynthesis process. The last remaining sources of oxygen are the streams and springs that may be at the lake bottom. On lakes subject to winter kill there are no feeder streams or they have ceased to flow owing to dry years or dams to control water for irrigation purposes. As winter progresses many organisms and fish deplete the oxygen supply, the last remaining oxygen being in the layer of water immediately under the ice.

Spring comes and the ice melts. The surface water warms until it reaches the temperature at which it becomes most dense. This dense water, containing the bulk of dissolved oxygen, now sinks through and mixes with the lower, oxygen-starved water, reducing the percentage of oxygen in the water. The oxygen-water ratio is now at a dangerous level and many fish will die before wind aeration, newly flowing streams or photosynthesis bring the oxygen to a normal saturation level.

In severe cases of winter kill the last oxygen is gone from the water before the ice melts and a total kill of all trout results.

Summer kill is caused by the factors of light penetration and water temperatures. As water temperature increases in summer heat it retains less and less oxygen until there is insufficient available to sustain the trout population. This condition rarely occurs since other circumstances are usually present to offset this catastrophe. There is normally sufficient wind to create circulation and aeration, and lakes free of algae with large beds of green weed growth contribute oxygen through photosynthesis during daylight hours. Dense amounts of suspended algae in the water will cut off much of the light, decreasing oxygen manufactured by plants.

In summer, fortunately, rarely do a sufficient number of adverse conditions prevail over a long enough period to create a serious problem.

## CHAPTER FIFTEEN

Rainbow Around the World

My experience of fly fishing for rainbow has been mainly in B.C., in particular the Kamloops area. It has been easy, therefore, to slip into the habit of referring to the rainbow trout as Kamloops. In the wider world of trout fishing, of course, the name by far most commonly used is rainbow. Naturally other species of trout respond to the skills of fly fishers described in the foregoing pages. But the rainbow is the king of the species and something of its history will interest those who appreciate its qualities.

It is not widely known that the rainbow originated on the Pacific Coast of North America. Its existence elsewhere on the continent and throughout the world is owed to transplanting programs carried on since 1874, using stock from northern California, Oregon and, more recently, British Columbia. Early fish and game authorities knew they could do no greater favor to trout fishermen than to make these handsome game fish available wherever they could survive on a self-sustaining basis.

A few sport fishermen from Britain and the eastern United States followed the pioneers, whose interest in stream fish was frankly that of meat hunters. It was easier for fur trappers, miners and loggers to take salmon or trout from streams than from lakes and the techniques used favored the largest poundage of fish with the least expenditure of time and effort. As more sophisticated people visited and inhabited the American West with the coming of the railways, the noble art of the fly fisher began to be practiced in California. The fame of this novel red sided, Shasta, or California, trout grew apace.

Inevitably the idea of transplanting fertilized eggs of these lusty, hard-hitting fighters with their colorful markings so different from native cutthroat, speckled or brown trout, and with their capability of topping 20 pounds, would get attention.

The first plantings of record occurred in 1874 and 1875 as a private undertaking. Seth Green of the Caledonia Hatchery, New York, incubated eggs obtained from Campbell Creek in the McCloud River system of north-

NATIVE RANGE OF
THE RAINBOW TROUT

1) *kamloops*
2) *whitehousei*
3) *beardsleei*
4) *gairdneri*
5) *masoni*
6) *newberryi*
7) *rivularis*
8) *stonei, shasta*
9) *aquilarum*
10) *smaragdus*
11) *regalis*
12) *iridea (irideus)*
13) *gilberti*
14) *whitei, roosevelti*
15) *rosei*
16) *aguabonita*
17) *evermanni*
18) *nelsoni*
19) *gilae*
20) *chrysogaster*

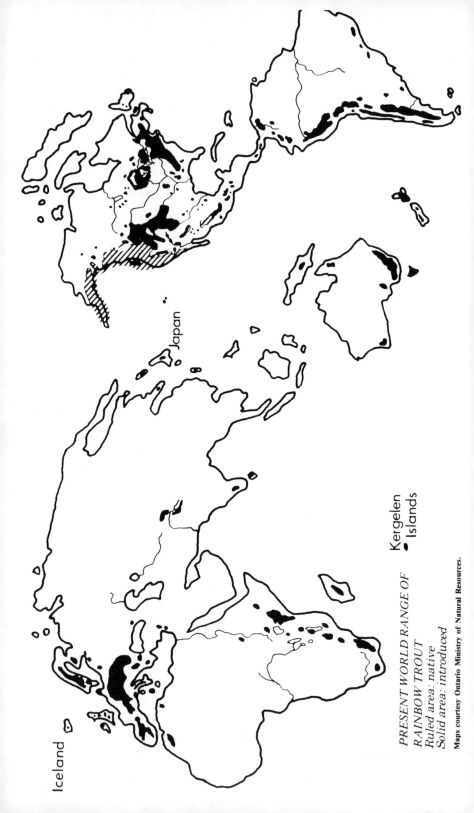

Iceland

Japan

Kergelen
Islands

PRESENT WORLD RANGE OF
RAINBOW TROUT
Ruled area: native
Solid area: introduced

Maps courtesy Ontario Ministry of Natural Resources.

ern California. By 1885, from this stock, nearly 9 million fingerlings had been released in New York State.

The Great Lakes area received its first eggs of the so-called California, or Shasta, trout in 1876 from the McCloud River through the enterprise of Daniel Fitzhugh, Jr. In 1878 there was a transfer of yearling McCloud River rainbow to the Northville Hatchery, located on the Rouge River in Michigan.

All the rainbow trout now indigenous to the Great Lakes system and to other streams and lakes of the Midwest did not evolve from this beginning. But even after the United States Fish Commission took over and operated the Northville Hatchery in 1880 the eggs incubated were from the McCloud River. Two of the principal actual sources were Crooks (now Green) Creek and Campbell Creek.

Not only New York and Michigan but also Pennsylvania, Wisconsin and Minnesota began with the McCloud River strain in the early 1880s. Thus there was a concentration of this breed of rainbow initially in the entire northeastern area of the United States and in the lake and river systems of the Midwest.

Between 1888 and the mid 1890s the California Fish Commission collected rainbow eggs on the Klamath River and incubated them in a hatchery on the headwaters of the Sacramento River. From this hatchery brood trout went to supplement stocking plans for various regions, including Michigan and New York.

Ontario's program of rainbow trout stocking first related to incubating eggs obtained from Bath, New York, for the Canada Department of Marine and Fisheries, with races of rainbow artificially developed at Port Arthur on Lake Superior and Southampton on Lake Huron. Practical programs with eggs of Kamloops trout did not begin in Ontario until 1934. From then until 1937 the Ontario government imported eggs from British Columbia and these furnished the nucleus of brood stocks successfully established. A fall-spawning strain from Minnesota was also introduced in 1934. This introduction, however, was decades after the first California strains of rainbow had gradually populated many of the streams and lakes tributary to the Great Lake systems.

While the newly naturalized rainbow, with access to the Great Lakes inland seas, quickly developed anadromous patterns of life resembling the migrations to the sea of their ancestor rainbow races of the Western watershed, rainbow populations also have developed in land-locked situations. These tend to require frequent hatchery plantings to maintain their attractiveness to sportsmen.

## CHAPTER SIXTEEN

Rainbow Age and Size

The range of age for a Kamloops, or rainbow, trout may be approximately established if it is remembered that under normal conditions of food availability the fish adds just about a pound a year to its weight. It is customary to refer to the rainbow as a steelhead when it has reached 20 inches in length.

The sea-run, mature rainbow of coastal waters returning to spawn as a steelhead is not dealt with in this work on lake fly fishing as it is not a prospect for sport in that environment. It may occasionally strike at a flasher when angry while passing through a lake on its way to a spawning stream. But it is obvious from experience of the fishing fraternity over many years that the ocean-fed steelhead in a lake is intent on its reproducing cycle in some suitable gravel bed. It does not linger to feed on insects. When its spawning function is discharged it loses little time in returning to its preferred surroundings in the sea.

There undoubtedly are instances of very large rainbow being taken in lakes which are not sea-run and which equal any of the ocean-feeding members of the species in size. Normally, the rainbow does not cannibalize if there is sufficient food for its natural dietary instincts in the lake it inhabits. Instances of huge land-locked trout being taken in such lakes suggests strongly that the trout has cannibalized its own species aggressively.

The largest fly-caught rainbow in B.C. is a 25-pound, 2-ounce one taken on a #8 Royal Coachman dry fly at Balfour on central Kootenay Lake in 1977. The largest rainbow ever weighed in B.C. — and quite likely the world — came from Jewel Lake near Greenwood in southern B.C. Although it wasn't caught on a fly, the background story is interesting.

It began about 1895 when a Swiss prospector, Louis Bosshart, staked claims on the lake and named one of them "Jewel." The claims proved rich in gold, with some silver and silica. Development proceeded and by 1913 gold bricks were being poured on the site. The rest of the story is told

Above left: At 48 and 56 pounds these rainbow from Jewel Lake, below, could be the world's largest. They were, however, gaffed rather than sport caught.

Above right: A 48-pound rainbow caught in Jewel Lake in the 1930s by unknown U.S. anglers. Fishermen shouldn't rush to the lake, however, since today its fish are under five pounds.

in an article written by Gladys M. Floyd for the Boundary Historical Society's excellent *10th Annual Report*:

"During this period, George White was one of the miners and his wife, Maria, was the cook. One evening in August, 1913 George took a stroll down to the lake after supper and stopped cold in his tracks when he saw dark shadows moving in the clear water. They were huge fish the like of which George had never before seen. He ran back up the hill to the blacksmith shop and grabbed a gaff — a large hook of some description — then sped back down to the lake where he landed two huge trout, one weighing in 56 pounds and the other at 48 pounds. Fortunately, Charles A. Banks was present to record White's catch on film.

"Until about the mid-1940s some of the jumbo trout continued to be caught from time to time. There appears to be no definitive record of how many were taken or the exact weights involved. Some may have been almost as large as the two taken by George White in 1913. One taken by a Spokane angler on sporting tackle is reported to have weighed in at over 50 pounds.

"A few times during the 1930s while the mine was operating, mysterious blasts blew out the dam at the foot of the lake, allowing fish to escape. The stream supplied water for the Floyd ranch on Highway 3 and on one occasion my brother Jim caught a 30-36″ trout in the irrigation ditch.

"Not being an expert on either mining or fishing, I can only pass on the speculation of others that the tailings pond found its ways into the lake and that the cyanide in it poisoned the large trout. I suppose this theory is as valid as any other guess. In any event none have been caught recently."

Kootenay Lake has yielded B.C.'s largest officially recognized rainbow on a fly.

Conclusion

Fly fishing is a combination of art and science. The manipulation of rod and line in a manner that will impart a natural movement to the imitation being fished is an art that is required only after practice and observation of the naturals. The closer one can approach this natural movement peculiar to each order of insect the greater one's chances of success. It becomes a science when the angler becomes interested in the "why" of the many aspects of fish and insect behavior. This study can become as interesting and absorbing as the actual fishing — and often much more rewarding. As one gains in knowledge, fishing success comes easier and the fisherman becomes more and more selective of the size and quality of fish taken.

The quiet relaxing atmosphere of a boat at anchor when only the waterfowl and the occasional plop of a rising fish intrude on one's placid thoughts is a rare and valued interlude in today's world of hustle and bustle. Tensions and frustrations can be forgotten entirely in a few relaxing days on the quiet waters of one of our many trout lakes. To sit and watch the sun set in its ever changing beauty can only add to the pleasure of this great sport. Finally, the gastronomical joy of a freshly caught trout is a reward not to be overlooked when weighing the merits of fly fishing as opposed to other forms of sport.

Fresh trout — fried, baked or prepared in many other ways — is just one of the pleasures of fish camp life. A smoked trout taken out on the lake for lunch with a thermos of tea, coffee or perhaps a bottle of beer is an experience not soon forgotten.

As one becomes aware of the insects on which fish feed it naturally comes to mind, "What microscopic organisms must these insects feed on?" With this question in mind any intelligent person soon realizes the delicacy of the environmental balance and becomes increasingly conscious of the effects of pollution not only on the sport of fly fishing but on all outdoor activities.

As a civilization we have reduced the fish potential in, or even destroyed, thousands of lakes and streams. Logging, mining, and other industrial activity, massive hydro dams and acid rain all have a cumulative effect on the environment. Nor are anglers blameless. Those who cut trees along the lakeshore for firewood, introduce illegal species into lakes, keep spawners, take more than their limit, leave garbage and similar abuses are part of the problem. A government that permits so much water to be diverted from streams that they become useless for spawning and refuses to allocate proper funds to maintain the fisheries resource is another. But possibly the biggest peril facing trout is apathy among anglers.

To preserve for our children the outdoor life we enjoy is a responsibility not to be taken lightly. In organizations such as the B.C. Wildlife Federation, the British Columbia Federation of Flyfishers and the Steelhead Society, anglers are battling pollution, damage to streams and other grave problems that imperil the future of rainbow trout.

Unfortunately, only a minority of the province's several hundred thousand anglers belong to such organizations. The majority are passive. If, instead, they joined the struggle to protect the fishery resource they would help ensure that not only their children but also all future generations will have quality fishing into the foreseeable future.

May success and joy be yours.

Jacko, one of over 400 lakes within a day's drive of Kamloops.

CHUCKWAGON RACING: Calgary Stampede's Half Mile of Hell

Four wagons behind 16 galloping horses chased by 16 outriders makes chuckwagon racing one of the world's most dangerous sports. Born at the Calgary Stampede in 1923, its heritage is the rangeland of the Canadian West. At the first chuckwagon race prize money was $275. By the 1980s it was $170,000. Today's races are so competitive that a one-second penalty can lose an outfit the $20,000 winner-take-all final heat.

Action-packed historical and current photos, four-color covers. $4.95

THE PICK OF THE NEIGHBOURHOOD PUBS: A Guided Tour in British Columbia

To make their selection the authors visited every pub accessible by road — travelling over 25,000 miles. Here are some 100 of the best. There are pubs on the water's edge, pubs with views, pubs with fine food, pubs with good entertainment and pubs which brew their own beer.

Scores of maps and photos, four-color covers, 160 pages of pub information and lore, including historical background. $9.95

GHOST TOWNS OF MANITOBA

In the 1880s settlers began to trickle into southern Manitoba, finding a vast open country where "a man could plow a furrow a mile long and never strike a stone." Soon towns by the score were born, all brimming with optimism but most fated to become only memories. Here is the story of Manitoba City, Bender Hamlet, Bannerman, Odanah, Asessippi, Ewart, and many other communities now only a pasture or a ploughed field.

Over 100 photos, four-color covers. 160 pages. $9.95

WHITE SLAVES OF THE NOOTKA

On March 22, 1803, while anchored in Nootka Sound on the West Coast of Vancouver Island, the *Boston* was attacked by "friendly" Nootka Indians. Twenty-five of her 27 crew were massacred, their heads "arranged in a line" for survivor John Jewitt to identify. Jewitt and another survivor became 2 of 50 slaves owned by Chief Maquina, never knowing what would come first — rescue or death.

The account of their ordeal, published in 1815, remains remarkably popular. New Western Canadian edition, well illustrated. 128 pages. $8.95

GO FISHING WITH THESE BEST SELLING TITLES

HOW TO CATCH SALMON — BASIC FUNDAMENTALS

The most popular salmon book ever written. Information on trolling, rigging tackle, most productive lures, proper depths, salmon habits, how to play and net your fish, downriggers, where to find fish.

Sales over 120,000. 176 pages. $4.95

HOW TO CATCH SALMON — ADVANCED TECHNIQUES

The most comprehensive advanced salmon fishing book available. Over 200 pages crammed full of how-to tips and easy-to-follow diagrams. Covers all popular salmon fishing methods: mooching, trolling with bait, spoons and plugs, catching giant chinook, and much more.

A continuing best seller. 256 pages. $5.95

HOW TO CATCH CRABS: How popular is this book? This is the 10th printing. 114 pages. $3.50

HOW TO CATCH BOTTOMFISH: Revised and expanded. $3.95

HOW TO CATCH SHELLFISH: Updated 4th printing. 144 pages. $3.95

HOW TO CATCH TROUT by Lee Straight, one of Canada's top outdoorsmen. 144 pages. $3.95

HOW TO COOK YOUR CATCH: Cooking seafood on the boat, in a camper or at the cabin. 7th printing. 192 pages. $3.95

FLY FISH THE TROUT LAKES: Everything you need to know about fly fishing B.C.'s lakes by Jack Shaw, a master angler who lives at Kamloops in B.C.'s famous trout country. Well illustrated. $6.95